Guidance
from the
Universe

Guidance
from the
Universe

Hopeful Messages
for Everyday Challenges

Jill Amy Sager

SHE WRITES PRESS

Published 2025
Printed in the United States of America
Print ISBN: 978-1-64742-754-2
E-ISBN: 978-1-64742-755-9
Library of Congress Control Number: 2024917352

For information, address:
She Writes Press
1569 Solano Ave #546
Berkeley, CA 94707

Interior Design by Tabitha Lahr

She Writes Press is a division of SparkPoint Studio, LLC.

For Clara and all my ancestors
who carried me here.

Contents

Preface

The Journey Begins

I was twelve, the year of Woodstock. I didn't go, but I wanted to be with all those untamed wild spirits reshaping archaic ways of thinking. My inclination toward unconventional ways of moving through the world came naturally to me. It seemed as if my affinity for being out of step with society's expectations was preordained . . . planted in my DNA at the time of conception. Maybe it was.

I came out of the womb with one leg shorter than the other. Being different, out of sync with the status quo, shaped my beginning and was compounded at age nine when I had surgery to correct the leg-length discrepancy that left me more disabled. By age twelve, scoliosis curved my spine so far to the right that my misshapen silhouette became an embarrassment, causing me further emotional and physical distress.

My inability to fit into societal norms meant I identified as an outsider. This permitted me to chart my course—a path I might not have had the courage to follow otherwise.

This book captures the highlights of that path and the insights I gained through my healing process to help you along with yours. My intention is to demonstrate how you have the power to change your life for the better with just a simple shift in perspective provided by words from Guidance, who inspired me to share this wisdom with you.

The alternative trajectory I chose for my life suited me, but it wasn't always easy.

I fell in love at fourteen with a girl, then hitched cross-country with a boyfriend that I later dumped to come out as a lesbian. After forty-plus years of identifying as gay, I wed Johnny. As conventional as that may sound, marrying a man went against everything I knew and went against everything my relatives and lesbian community expected of me at the time.

I received my first deck of Tarot cards as a gift in my early twenties. Fifteen years later, I heard a voice.

When I started receiving messages from the Universe, I knew they weren't coming from me because I am neither scholarly nor have I studied spiritual ideology or philosophy. Over the years, the voice grew stronger and more pronounced. So, although I have been a professional practitioner of the Tarot for forty years, it is this wise invisible source that I can't explain—but can't deny—that mostly comes through these days. I named the entity "Guidance" because the word means "help."

When I do a reading, I am often asked, "Who is the 'they' you are referring to?" While it isn't an easy question to answer, I think of Guidance like a radio frequency that's always on. This channel of love is what I tune into.

I realize the messages I receive aren't limited to a specific entity. That's why I refer to Guidance using plural pronouns. Love isn't a limited "thing." Love is expansive. Therefore, as much as I've tried to put Guidance in a box by identifying what, who, or where these messages come from, I am only left to wonder.

I intended to be something other than a go-between for spirit or a professional Tarot reader. Offering readings never crossed my mind as a vocation to pursue. However, when my sister introduced my skill to her friends years ago, word spread.

Today, I have clients worldwide and host free live weekly readings on social media. Through my "Moments of Contemplation" subscriber list, Substack, and social media sites, I share Guidance's wisdom and a few musings of my own.

Guidance came into my life unexpectedly. I had no idea that working with Tarot cards would be a point of entry—a way to increase my intuition and open the door to the larger Universe. I discovered this by accident.

It happened during a Tarot reading. The Queen of Cups looked pregnant, which is not indicative of this card. When I mentioned it to my client, she affirmed that her question and concern had everything to do with motherhood.

From that day forward, I trusted my sixth sense. But one incident, in particular, would change my life forever. During an emotionally challenging period, I saw a diminutive figure I can only describe as a tiny Tinker-Bell-like creature.

The visitor frightened me initially, but I felt comforted during our few minutes together. With a gentle, soothing voice, she whispered words that seemed to float in the air from her lips to my ear. She told me everything would be all right, and I would survive the insurmountable pain and loss. Then she disappeared. What remained was my belief in her declaration.

That apparition never appeared again. Her presence, however, extended my awareness about what may lay beyond the veil of everyday existence.

From the beginning, I allowed for Guidance, because like the Tarot, their love, kindness, and support came through. Yet their lessons were broader and wiser. I became wiser by listening.

I came to realize how I was responsible for my destruction or happiness based on what I thought, how I felt, and how I acted.

Through Guidance's teachings, I learned to pay attention to my internal struggles, to thoughts weighing me down and emotions pulsing through me that caused me to suffer.

No matter their message, the underlying foundation of their wisdom is that I accept and love myself. Their insights enabled me to live a more fulfilled life. This gift is available for you, too, and is the main reason I decided to bring their wisdom to light.

Throughout my adult life, Guidance steps in whenever I feel low and at my worst. Like a great coach, their enlightened words keep me on track. With this offering, their encouragement is available to you like I've been encouraged all these years.

They remind us to live to our fullest potential. This by no means involves some grand plan for our lives. Living better means we love ourselves more.

Guidance offers us the tools to make that possibility more realized. They asked me to share those tools with you so you can access the benefits.

Now, I'm no guru, nor am I "special." I just decided to pay attention to the loving wisdom of the Universe. I have experienced firsthand the life-altering value of Guidance's core message: to "know thyself." But let me clarify it: by no means do I think that self-awareness is an earth-shattering revelation.

Countless people on social media and others are writing books and offering workshops hawking self-love and motivating us to feel better, do better, and live happier. Look at how long Oprah has been encouraging this agenda. Not to mention Socrates, who philosophized that happiness could be achieved not by material possessions but by what we know.

Therefore, pointing our finger inward to gain the most out of life is a message that always remains the same. This book came about not because the concept is new but because I felt strongly that Guidance's unique voice would inspire you in a brand-new way.

When I returned to my journals to type up what Guidance had given me, I didn't expect to find so much meaty goodness. I had forgotten how much material there was. Yet here it all is. Topics galore.

We all grapple with jealousy, worry, and failure. We wonder about money's influence on our lives and how to forgive or be less judgmental.

Well, Guidance lays out how to tackle those times when we need help figuring out what to do. They walk us through these topics—thirty in this book alone—so we gain insights that move us forward with greater clarity.

My association with Guidance has been life-changing. This is why I offer you the opportunity to read my stories on each topic—to demonstrate how I used Guidance's wisdom to grow beyond behaviors that no longer serve me. I think Guidance can help you too.

Ultimately, what Guidance wants is for us to flourish. They help us achieve this by gently focusing on the suffering we can cause ourselves.

I hope these insights will dislodge many internal blocks that get in your way so you too, can move from where you are to where you want to be: happier, freer, and more content, with a life of choices that better suit you. Ultimately, the kindness we show ourselves offers the possibility that our caring nature can rise. In this way we'll get better at caring for each other and our planet.

This book is filled with wisdom to support you on that journey.

With love and deep gratitude,
Jill Amy

Introduction

I don't claim to have all the answers. What I do have are my experiences, so I included them. I wrote personal stories on each of the thirty topics in this book to reflect how I used Guidance's words to positively reshape my life, thinking my process might support yours.

I refer to Guidance in plural form because I feel their divine presence with a loving potency so expansive that I prefer to use the pronoun "they" instead of "it."

Guidance's wisdom appears in italics throughout this book with a unique communication style. They do not always speak to us with perfect grammar. So, if you find some messages hard to understand, allow your unconscious to sift through them. In this way, you will discover the nuggets of gold that resonate with you.

Each chapter finishes with "Reflections," which offer thought-provoking questions to jump-start your internal musings. You might find it helpful to keep a journal, as I did, to deepen your understanding.

I suggest you read this book from cover to cover for context as your way to become familiar with Guidance's voice and mine. Then, reread specific passages or chapters as you need.

I have always believed that the information from Guidance offers what any good self-help book would. This means there will be passages that speak to your truth, the soul of you, while other ideas won't strike you as worthy.

Ultimately, you are your best teacher. Trust in your intuitive knowing. Therefore, take what you need and leave the rest.

I hope you find inspiration in these pages, and beyond that, I hope you enjoy the read.

Each step you take in consciousness informs your other steps.
We know this process isn't easy.
We also know that your availability to self for self is what you desire.
All the love that exists in this world resides in you,
and awareness of this love is your true calling.

————◆‡◆————

1. Awareness

Awareness is all.

IX

THE HERMIT.

There is no greater gift to self than being self-aware. Acceptance of who you are brings freedom and a lightness of being.

There are so many who can show you how to become aware, but nobody can take you there. It is up to you to decide that awareness is the way to live.

Each of you will find your way toward consciousness to be awake to who you are. For that is your birthright, to know yourself better. Trusting what you know about yourself is the best of what is possible.

Acceptance of who you are brings a lightness of being.

When you are awake, you cannot be led by habits; old fears cannot lead you. You cannot be led by what was ingrained in you as a child, and others cannot lead you.

Being awake is finding who you are each moment, leading you to peace.
So you are led to love.
So you are led to be the person you want to live with.

Accepting who you are in each moment is truth . . . to acknowledging yourself without judgment is what elevates your life. Acceptance of who you are, without the strain of self-doubt, without the woe of self-apology, without the need to self-punish, is consciousness for you.

How can one be against self?

Decide to be awake. Learn how to be awake. This habit will bring you *more of what you want because you are more of yourself.*

Mindful awareness is the key; in this, the riches of each moment will bring what you have to offer, what you have to give, and will bring you deeply to you, so you'll be led astray no more.

Welcome self to self. Embrace self with self. Nothing matters more in this lifetime.

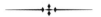

Before my dad died, he and I would check in about once a week by phone because we lived on opposite coasts. Our conversations were short. When he asked how I was, I said "fine" even when I wasn't or if things weren't going well—like when my landlord evicted me, and I had to scramble to find a new place to live.

My dad was an obsessive worrier. I learned to spare him (and myself) from any aspects of my life that might make him anxious. This meant many topics remained off the table. I avoided sharing a mild cold because he would grill me, fearing my cough would lead to pneumonia.

On one Saturday, while I was living in Berkeley, he called. He caught me right after finishing lunch. As usual, I kept our conversation light. We didn't talk long, maybe ten minutes tops.

When I hung up, I sank into a depressive, melancholy mood. My plan that afternoon included walking the two blocks to Peet's Coffee Shop. Instead, I laid down on the couch, ready to zone out in front of the TV.

On weekends, I often stood in line at Peet's flagship store to grab a cup of coffee while taking in the warm sunshine Berkeley was known for. I lazily roamed around my neighborhood, strolling past the boutique shops on Shattuck Avenue. This included the famed Chez Panisse restaurant, where the daily menu was posted near the front door. I always looked, fantasizing that I could afford to eat there one day.

Maybe I became aware of the gloominess that hung around me that afternoon because it starkly contrasted with the fun I had anticipated. Or maybe because I felt melancholy most days, I never made the connection that my dad's calls drastically affected my mood.

Whatever the reason, I noticed for the first time what had been taking place for years: conversations with my dad left me feeling sad.

I leaped off the couch. I ignored the TV remote that sat inches away. I grabbed my keys, locked the front door, and bounced up the street toward Peet's.

From that moment forward, whenever my dad and I spoke on the phone, a warning bell went off in my head—a reminder that I might become depressed after the call ended. It was like having my private navigational system.

This insight about my dad brought forth an image of Pinocchio when he was a wooden puppet manipulated by someone else—or, in my case, at the mercy of unconscious habits, knee-jerk reactions, or unexamined feelings pulling at my strings. My new awareness made me feel more alive.

Guidance says that once we are awake to a situation, there is no going back to being asleep about the particulars. Guidance likens this recognition to how we remember the taste of a great meal. This is what I have come to experience. My epiphanies are exactly like the best plate of carbonara pasta I have tasted—so seared in my memory, there is no way to forget the effect on me. When it came to my dad, I was never blind-sided again when I hung up the phone.

Guidance's core message, no matter the topic, is always about love. Therefore, I must be more self-accepting to be more of what love asks of me. To be more self-accepting, I must become more self-aware.

Being "awake" is like flipping on a light switch so I see my brightness. That means all of me, whatever is true—the good, the bad, and the ugly. This isn't always easy, but Guidance's message about mindful awareness continues to resonate. The gift is recognizing myself with clarity. Clarity enables me to make healthier, more advantageous choices.

This ongoing process of resurrection changes my perceptions, allowing me to accept the challenges I face, while I take better care of myself as I face them.

Yet, even with the benefits I experience by being "awake," I have no illusion that I am capable of mindful awareness 24-7. That goal seems unattainable. All I am capable of is tying my awakened moments together more often. My wish for you is the same.

Reflections

Many of us aren't fully present as we go through our day. We remain unaware of our motives, actions, fears, and sometimes even the reasons we made a specific decision. The phrase "on autopilot" comes to mind.

Becoming aware—which can be done in hindsight too—takes patience, practice, and a willingness most of all. Emotions are a good entry point for becoming more mindful and, therefore, more "awake."

Take time with these questions. Awareness is about what we discover by being vulnerable and honest.

1. What would you gain by being more aware of your emotional barometer?
2. Are there times when you feel more asleep, like you are going through the motions?
3. What might be different if you were more aware? Present in the moment more often?

Awareness changes how we view ourselves and is the first step toward having the authentic life so many of us want, yet, at times, can feel elusive.

Guidance makes the case that "awareness," this living with conscious connection, frees us to be who we truly are. Authenticity means we aren't hiding from others, but more importantly, we aren't hiding from ourselves—good enough reason to pursue a more awakened self.

2. Emotions

One can decide if an emotion is good or bad,
but, in humans, emotions are.

THE MOON.

Emotions are the way to your heart—your way to love. Emotions are your true path to enlightenment. So, how has it come to be that humans deny what is most precious to each of you—your emotional core.

You were created in the totality of all things, and this includes emotions. Do not hide from feelings.

It is only avoidance that brings harm.

Feelings are what each of you carries in your soul. Each of you will feel anger, hate, jealousy, joy, love. Feeling these is no mistake. You are human. Emotions are within you, a profound gift to each of you in this lifetime.

For most people, the impulse is to act on their feelings. But we ask that you first reserve time with an emotion, for this space is where you can decide what to do with the feeling. And to do that, you must first sit and wait to discover what it is you truly feel.

This is what you must learn. It is simple, but humans need to spend time in this space.

Humans have the gift of discernment, and your mind was created for this.

When you feel hate or love in your body, it is your mind that can discern between the two. But to do this, we ask that you recognize that all emotions stand on neutral ground, without judgment.

Emotions are transformed easily in a moment when you notice your tightened heart of hate. Your fearful mistrust of love. Your scourging sickness of shame or sadness that clogs your day. When you are privy to that, then you can ask the Universe for the strength to release the anger you carry that hurts your heart. To cry into the love that you want. To witness the shame that robs you. It is then that you gain clarity.

Sitting with your feelings allows them to surface, so you feel their power but not their power over you.

We ask that you accept all your emotions as great teachers.

Emotions are like nature, which shows that everything has a dark and light side like day and night. Look at the day and night of your emotions. Seeing that what looks negative has another side that is positive. Discover what you can learn about the self by seeing all sides of your emotions. This will bring you closer to you and, in so doing, you will learn much about self. And when you notice self, love can come to visit.

My mother and brother have been a tight twosome since he came out of her womb five years after my birth. When Daniel was a toddler, their nightly rituals of cuddling and goofing around created squeals of giggles coming from his bedroom. This left me feeling rejected by my mom, who spent more time having fun with him than me.

One evening, after saying goodnight to my brother, my mother entered the bedroom I shared with my sister, and, after she plopped herself on my bed, I climbed onto her lap. Looking back, I was jealous of her relationship with my brother, but at seven years old, I didn't understand this. Instead, I asked my mom if she loved me.

She looked at me, with her eyes wide in shocked disbelief, and said I should stop being silly. Of course, she loved me. Then, without warning, she spread her knees, dropping me to the floor. I landed with both feet on the ground, more confused than satisfied.

For the entire time I lived with my parents until I left home at eighteen, I don't remember feeling emotionally validated. When

I reached adulthood, my ability to understand my emotions, let alone name them, was on par with my inability to comprehend math. I had no aptitude for either.

I was almost thirty when I realized that snorting cocaine, getting drunk, or watching TV in excessive amounts were ways I avoided my emotions, so I sought weekly counseling. To enter my therapist's office, I had to ring a buzzer. On more than one occasion, she left me standing on the street because she was a no-show for our appointment.

After one of these incidents, while I sat in my usual place, snuggling up to the right arm of her long couch, my therapist asked if I felt angry or hurt that she had forgotten me. One or both of those emotions would have been appropriate, but at the time, I couldn't access how I felt. I told her I was fine.

It wasn't that I didn't express emotions. On the contrary, I became angry, I cried, and I laughed. But I was like a two-year-old who showed outward expressions without the ability to name which emotion had surfaced.

This disconnect with my feelings prevented me from being vulnerable, which meant my intimate partners and friends didn't know me because I didn't know myself. For many years, I lived with an internal struggle, as if I were two people—one whose emotions got the better of me, while the other had no clue what I truly felt or why I reacted the way I did.

Like the time I had an awkward encounter with a friend. We were finishing our meal at a restaurant when she left rather suddenly. I was consumed by thoughts that I must have said something to offend her. As the days went on, my irritability and shame grew. I wanted to understand.

Guidance offered advice.

Sit still. How does your body feel?

I tried doing what they asked. I felt snowed under, heavily weighted by self-loathing. I recognized depression, married with the troubling thought that I felt like a bad person. I tried but couldn't release the thought. I wanted to understand. I settled back to focus on Guidance's question again. How did my body feel? I stopped thinking. I forced myself to listen. What was my body telling me?

Every part of me buzzed like a fidgety child. Jumpy. On edge. I couldn't sit still.

My discomfort grew. My anxiety persisted like an annoying mosquito, returning repeatedly, no matter how many times I swatted at it to go away. I mentally pushed and pulled at the tension. I tried denying what I felt while feeling so much.

Then I wondered what would happen if I sat with all the agitation, all the rumbling, and all the fretting. What would happen if I accepted the struggle raging within me? And that's what I did. The acceptance relaxed my distress. Within moments, a memory surfaced.

I was six years old, watching my mom apply makeup in front of the bathroom mirror. As I stood behind her, I stuck out my tongue, assured that her back protected my action. I remember feeling angry, although I don't remember why.

She left the bathroom in a huff without saying a word. I had been caught. Through my panic, I heard the familiar creak of my dad's closet door open, then the ting-a-ling sound of swinging belt buckles, a sure sign she was choosing a leather strap to smack me with. That wasn't the first or last time I was physically punished for doing something that upset her.

On the morning my tongue left the safety of my mouth, my mom and I did not discuss what caused my anger. She didn't use it as a teachable moment about how to express my frustration more appropriately. Nor did either of us admit that we had hurt each other.

Being physically punished when I did something wrong was a normal part of my upbringing. I knew this. But reliving the incident brought unexpected insight, as deeply rooted as an ancient perennial plant whose tightly-bound clumps need to be pulled apart so new life can form. As I pondered this, I pulled apart years of tangled emotional neglect so new life could emerge for me, too.

My mom's punishments came with a force that quieted whatever I felt. The striking message from that day forward was that I was a "bad" person for doing something "bad." No wonder I felt out of sorts anytime I had an inkling I screwed up, as I had with my friend. Acting badly and being a bad person was mixed in my psyche, a shame deeply held in my body, swallowing any sense of goodness in me.

This awareness freed me from the negative thoughts I had about myself. I turned back into the responsible adult I appreciated. I called my friend to ask if I had said something to offend her.

Learning to discern my feelings and honor them meant I honored myself. When I became curious about the overwhelming feeling of self-hate after being with my friend, I learned a great deal about myself. I got closer to what makes me tick. And I experienced what Guidance points to so wisely . . . that our emotions are an important snapshot into who we are.

Some emotions are harder for me to grapple with than others, but coming to terms with my real truth is worth the effort. Like unwrapping a present bound with too much tape, it might take me a while to tear away the layers. But when I persevere, I ultimately find the gifts, long hidden and worth the reveal.

Reflections

Guidance points out that our feelings are natural; therefore, being in touch with our emotions should be second nature. Unfortunately, this is not the case for many of us. Denying or judging or being numb to our emotions is often the norm.

Closeted emotions, however—the ones we ignore or stuff—still affect our thoughts and actions. We have all experienced this. The spiritual lesson "what we resist persists" comes to mind.

Emotions we don't deal with—those we can't get a handle on or refuse to accept—plague us anyway and undermine the healing we seek.

All emotions have something to tell you, so judging yourself about anything you feel is about as useful as cutting with a dull knife. Be kind to yourself. Embrace what you discover while answering these questions.

1. What were you taught about emotions as a child that might hinder or help your growth?
2. Which emotions are you able to accept? Which ones do you negatively judge, deny, or avoid in others or yourself?
3. Can you identify where a specific emotion, such as anger, for example, lands in your body? And if so, what happens when you stay with the feeling? Does the feeling shift?

Guidance once told me that "they" have no emotions. That on the other side (if there is one and we get there), we, too, will be void of feelings. If that's true and we don't have emotional capacity after we die, why squander the gift here?

The ability to discern and define our emotions makes us human. Therefore, it makes sense to become knowledgeable about our feelings and embrace the full range of emotions, so we experience true intimacy with ourselves and each other.

3. Anger

Anger isn't cruel. Anger isn't harsh.
Anger is only an emotion.

Anger does not want to hurt you, nor does it want to hurt others. But it does ask for your attention.

Anger explodes with a passion and a force that one must recognize. That explosive price is yours and no one else's. All emotions teach you, and the more you understand anger, the less explosive it will be.

Be wise with anger. Allow it to teach you. As you look at anger, it speaks. It has value in your life.

Anger is a release. It is a release to remove toxins.

Anger expels what is harmful to the body, mind, and soul, which is much needed.

Anger is not your enemy; it is your friend. But who among you wants to befriend this emotion? Who among you only sees how anger hurts you? Who among you only sees the destruction that it causes? But this is not anger. This is what anger does, not what anger is.

Anger is a volcano erupting at the surface, but there is so much more one does not see below. Below is what you must seek. Below is what you are called to understand. Below, for many, is born from past misgivings.

When one finds what is below anger, the anger is released, and then there is calm, and that is what we also want you to befriend.

Many can't sit with anger, but few try. Sit with anger. Ask anger what it wants. Find out what is below your anger. This practice is your way to release what hurts you.

Anger will always speak its wrath, but when you hold wrath for moments and pet its lovely head, it will fold in your arms and whisper its love.

Those of you who discover what is in anger's heart will release what is at its core and will understand that anger has no power—except to show you the power of love.

During a painful breakup with the woman I thought I would be married to for the rest of my life, a friend flew from San Francisco to Eugene to lend her support. Lyn wasn't with me long when she offered to give feedback about my behavior that might have contributed to the demise of the relationship.

By then, I had suffered three disappointing breakups. That list included Lyn, so her opinion had merit.

She didn't hold back. Lyn said that when I got angry, I acted like a mama bear protecting her cubs. She had experienced this unpleasantness, making it clear that my fierce attitude scared people away.

I became defensive. I argued that I had a right to spew my anger at a girlfriend or anyone who said or did something to infuriate me. But Lyn wouldn't have it.

She stated the obvious; mouthing off wasn't getting me what I wanted.

I grew up in a household where expressing anger was as common as eating breakfast. When I moved from my parents' home into my own, the quiet unnerved me. Only later did I recognize that I yelled at my roommates to ease my discomfort.

My dad's fury came on quickly, without warning. He bullied my brother and yelled at inanimate objects like the ketchup bottle when he couldn't find it in the fridge.

My mom was miserable in her marriage. She dealt with her bitterness by yelling at my dad and me. When she wasn't raging, she wore a permanent scowl on her face. Her venom bit me hard, and she never apologized for her outbursts.

Out of us three kids, I was the middle child who defied her. When I returned my mom's anger with anger, she punished me for acting the same way she did. Her hypocritical stance fueled my frustration and made me angrier.

By the time I left home at eighteen, anger was my go-to emotion. Like my mom, I released it righteously. I let my venom fly without apology, no matter the circumstance.

I once snapped at an ex-girlfriend because she didn't wash the head of lettuce to my liking. Of course, my fury had nothing to do with the lettuce. But back then, I couldn't contain the explosion of heat rising within me. No matter the reason, I lost control.

Even strangers didn't escape my wrath. Walking on a sidewalk in Manhattan one spring, I turned around to an unsuspecting man in broad daylight, yelling "Get the fuck away" because he followed too close behind me. Yes, that apple didn't fall far from the mother tree.

When Lyn left after the weekend to return to San Francisco, I wondered about her take on my anger. Guidance had this to say:

Anger has not been your enemy. It has much to tell you. It is yours to have and hold. So, we ask not that you cut it loose, but only that you listen when it beats deep inside, so you understand its lessons.

I had no idea what anger wanted to teach me, but I felt ready to open my mind to changing a behavior that had cost me dearly in relationships and self-esteem.

I read books about anger, took an anger management workshop, threw rocks in a river while screaming (a friend suggested this), and furiously smashed glass bottles into the pit at the county dump (another friend's suggestion), hoping to rid all the anger bubbling inside me. None of it worked. Any incident that made me feel volatile remained in my thoughts, like a playlist on repeat.

It wasn't until my husband and I were discussing a promotion that he needed to consider, that Guidance's advice—to contemplate my hostility, to be with it, get to know it—finally sank in.

Johnny and I sat in the kitchen finishing dinner when I badgered him to decide about the new position he had been offered at work. My voice was raised and grew louder. He left the room without a word, leaving a crater-size rift between us.

I scrubbed the dinner dishes with an intensity that surely might have broken one or two. I couldn't settle down. I felt out of sorts. I was seething. I knew this feeling.

Why was I fuming about a choice that he clearly had to make? My hostility toward Johnny seemed out of line, even to me.

I did what Guidance asked. I stood at the sink with my blood boiling while looking for answers. I hated feeling this out of control. I witnessed my discomfort, my suffering, and the suffering I caused Johnny.

After I washed the last pan, I knew what bothered me. I gathered myself with a few deep breaths and went into Johnny's office feeling calmer.

His eyes remained on the computer with his back to me. He didn't acknowledge my presence.

I gathered my nerve and offered him a sincere apology. Being humble didn't feel natural, but each word came from my heart, which made it easier to continue. My outburst was inappropriate, and I told him this. Taking responsibility lifted the weight of hurting him.

He turned around. His eyes softened. I sat down on the chair next to him. I began explaining what had caused my outburst.

For the past few weeks, Johnny moped around the house. After dinner, he went into his office without a word to me, closed the door, and didn't come out until bedtime when he grunted a goodnight and rolled over.

I knew his reclusiveness was to avoid the emotional turmoil he struggled with because he couldn't decide about the job offer. I had been understanding and supportive while denying the toll it took on me.

I realized how his isolating behavior reminded me of living with my parents, who were perpetually unhappy with their life. When they weren't fighting, they withdrew from each other and me. I spent long Saturdays in their house, making sure I didn't disturb my mother who hid in her bedroom behind closed doors while my dad was nowhere to be found.

I acknowledged Johnny's stress, but I let him know that the more he withdrew, the more alone I felt. My inability to connect with him and his refusal to connect with me scared me.

As the word "scared" left my lips, Johnny patted his thighs. I moved over to sit on his lap. I apologized again for getting angry at him. He apologized for being inattentive. We hugged each other tight, feeling lifted by the conversation and the love that connected us. We both felt better.

Guidance was right. Anger had something to teach me.

Lashing out was safer than admitting I felt hurt, scared, disappointed, or any number of emotions that left me vulnerable. Anger became my defense against powerlessness. I was a mama bear, all right, protecting myself.

That night, I took time in the kitchen to figure out what anger wanted to tell me. In so doing, I experienced an intimate, honest connection with myself that enabled me to be honest and intimate with Johnny. The upshot of all this growth is that I no longer make excuses for my ill behavior the way I used to.

Anger had been so problematic for me that when I started to heal my relationship with it, I figured the goal meant eradicating the feeling altogether. Instead, I discovered that seeing "red" is a warning sign and a powerful motivating force for self-reflection and change.

As Guidance promised, I do feel calmer when I take the time to understand what's triggering my anger. I used to believe that spewing anger was a righteous act. Now I know that feeling anger is a righteous emotion I can embrace and befriend. The irony is that I have become a less angry person.

Reflections

All of us have anger. Even people who don't express anger outwardly experience it. Whether anger is denied or expressed, it controls us and undermines our self-confidence.

Therefore, getting to the root of its germinating seed seems a more hopeful solution than vilifying or denying anger, since that only seems to fuel our destructive responses. Gaining intimacy with anger means we must first take steps toward learning its secrets.

1. Can you recall any messages you received about anger from those who raised you?
2. How does anger affect you physically? Can you identify where it sits in your body?
3. Do you think you have a healthy relationship with anger? If not, what would you like to change?

When we become mindful of our anger, we can discern the many ways anger harms and benefits us. After all, anger can be a motivating force for good. I have quit a few toxic jobs thanks to being in touch with my anger. Anger isn't our enemy. It's what we do with this emotion that hinders or helps our growth.

4. Surrender

Choose to surrender when all else is futile.

Humans are good at planning and deciding how things will go. Humans are less comfortable surrendering and trusting that all will work out despite what it is one may think or do.

Humans want to control. This is where they can become misguided.

Are you a donkey? Stubborn. Are you a goat? Ramming your head against a fence post that will never move. Why do humans make it harder than it has to be?

Tension is created when you cannot see a situation for what it is. When you hold onto something or someone so tightly to the way you think it has to be, then you are bound and blocked from your own well-being.

We are not saying to sit on your hands and do nothing.

We are saying that there are times when you must be ready to surrender.

To surrender when things don't go your way.

To surrender to how things are.

To trust more.

Trust that no matter what you want to happen or want to do, there is a better plan.

Visualize surrender like a boat floating downstream. When you stop pushing against the river, you allow for flow. And when you are in flow, the Universe and you can better work together to make any plan so.

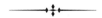

It was a rainy October when I broke my knee. Rain in the Pacific Northwest means mud. I took Spiral, my regal, eighty-five-pound chow-shepherd mix, for her usual romp in the dog park. We headed down a grass-covered embankment. I slipped and fell.

My left knee hasn't bent past forty-two degrees since childhood surgeries left me permanently disabled. When I hit the ground, that leg was caught beneath me. I heard a snap. My kneecap shattered, and tendons tore away from my muscles.

Surgery was the only option if I hoped to walk again. The operation proved a success, but the recovery would be challenging.

I couldn't put weight on my leg for three months. I couldn't drive. I hobbled around on crutches. This meant being home most of the time.

Under normal circumstances, I love lounging around. I wallow away the time guilt-free. Considering the number of friends who struggle with downtime, my ability to sit for hours doing nothing without pressuring myself to do otherwise is a marvel of upbringing I take pride in.

I inherited my laziness from my dad, who could spend all Sunday (and did) with the *New York Times* splayed around his feet while he napped in between sections. I have no doubt there will be many things I'll regret on my deathbed, but less relaxing won't be one.

That autumn, I had planned on finishing an instructional hand-drum book to send to publishers, but like my knee, that goal was shattered. As adept as I am at frittering away time when I feel at my best, my ability to accomplish absolutely zilch doesn't hold a candle to the times when I'm sick or laid up.

I can't concentrate when I'm not feeling well. Waiting for my knee to heal meant catching up on one more Netflix series.

I might excel at idleness, but my disappointment over the book taking a backseat would be an understatement. I felt cheated, convinced the Universe was against me. My inability to surrender to the derailed timeline fueled my daily frustration.

To seek answers, I went to my bookshelf to find Louise Hay's *You Can Heal Your Life* (Hay House Inc., 1984) to gain insight.

According to Ms. Hay, knee problems represent pride, ego, and the inability to give in. I was being stubborn, all right. Guidance's words also hit home.

Resistance becomes your inner struggle, and your inner struggles are far worse for you than any outer struggle.

My refusal to accept what happened was, in fact, causing inner conflict. I tried, then failed, to gather up steam to get my head back into finishing the book. But I couldn't do it. I gave in to the delay.

Surrendering to my circumstances gave me the peace I needed to focus on healing. Hay's words continued to resonate, prompting me to seek further answers. Had I been holding onto something that contributed to my fall in the first place?

I journaled for weeks. Then my answer came.

Lindsey and I had broken up years before, yet as I reread Hay's words about pride and ego and the inability to give in, I had to admit that there were moments in my day when I thought about the way she had left me for someone else. My ego took the same devastating hit each time.

When Lindsey told me she wanted to be with someone else, nothing I said or did could sway her from leaving me. It was a breakup born of betrayal. I was sideswiped without warning and left as roadkill.

With a broken knee that kept my ass stuck on the couch, I realized how I still held onto the troubling despair of feeling powerless against her decision. Did I enjoy reliving this hurt over and over?

I turned my view away from Lindsey and pointed it toward myself. I continually blamed her infidelity for the reason we broke up. Being a victim absolved me of taking responsibility.

I did more soul-searching. I recalled how she asked me repeatedly to deal with my anger. I never did. Throughout our seven years of living together, Lindsey got my wrath whether she deserved it or not. I remembered that while we were still together, she warned me on more than one occasion that she would leave me if it didn't get resolved.

What I had never done was surrender my smugness: confessing to my shortcoming, that I had a hand in the demise of our relationship meant wading through uncomfortable feelings of humiliation. Still, I also discovered it felt good to admit I was at fault. The clarity, the truth, set me free.

With my knee finally healed, I went for my last appointment with the surgeon. He told me to go home, shed the brace, and put full weight on my knee. My leg hadn't touched solid ground for three months.

My doctor had no answers about whether the knee's previous range of motion would return or whether I would be in worse shape. He advised me to continue using the crutches until the knee felt stable, cautioning it could take a few weeks.

Lindsey drove me home from the doctor. We had managed to stay friends, even though being around her reignited the pain of her leaving me. After uncovering my dysfunctional fog, I realized later that re-experiencing the sting of that breakup might have been why I stayed in touch with her.

When Lindsey and I entered my house, I asked her to stick around in case I had a problem. I sat on the couch while she watched from a chair across the room. I slowly unstrapped each Velcro strip, freeing my leg from the apparatus. I carefully put on a sock, avoiding knee bending, and reintroduced my left foot to its shoe.

I stood to take my first steps. Lindsey promised to help if I showed signs I might fall. We were both nervous.

I grabbed my crutches for support and put half my weight on the knee. Then I took another step. I had no pain. I took a few more steps. The knee showed no sign of weakness. The leg felt stable.

I put down the crutches. I walked around the living room, then into the kitchen. My knee's limited range of motion was the same as it had been before the break, but no worse. I strolled around my house as if the trauma never happened.

I won't deny I had a competent surgeon; I must give him props. But I have to give myself props too, for I healed so well without suffering long-term effects from the fall.

I surrendered to a truth I had been denying. Hay and Guidance were on target about how physical healing depends on many factors. Hay pointed me toward my inflexibility, and Guidance's wisdom bore out.

Surrendering frees us from the harm our tension creates.

I didn't talk to Lindsey that afternoon about my part in our breakup. That apology would come later. When I shut the door behind her, I faced my single life alone again. But the sadness and self-pity that usually lingered after we spent time together had vanished. Instead, I felt content to be living life on my terms.

That fall, I learned about surrender. I learned to give in, wave the white flag, and accept defeat gracefully. But giving in and giving up are not the same thing. And that winter, I returned to writing my book.

I can't say for certain what would have happened if I had stuck to my original deadline for finishing the manuscript. I know that surrendering to my situation—releasing the fixed timeline I had set—didn't negatively influence the outcome as I feared.

Shortly after completing the first draft, which took another year, I serendipitously met an influential person who offered me the opportunity to present the finished work to a well-respected New York publisher. Six months later, I sat in their office signing a book contract.

Reflections

There isn't a one-size-fits-all regarding what we surrender
to or why. Guidance suggests, however, that we investigate.

While I was nursing my knee, I surrendered my pride. I
surrendered the book's original timeline for being finished.
I surrendered to my true, sluggish nature. In each instance,
I felt better once I let go of "control." Surrendering doesn't
have to mean we give up. It means we trust what's in front
of us.

The next time you notice you're spinning your wheels
without a resolution, you might contemplate how fixated
you are about wanting things to be a certain way instead
of how it is.

1. What do you fear might be lost if you surrendered?
2. What might feel different if you surrendered?
3. What are the possible benefits of surrendering to
   what is?

I'm a headstrong person. Some friends might even
call me stubborn. To make matters worse, my astrological
sun sign in Aquarius means my default setting is "I know."
And boy, do I like to be right. With those fixed attributes,
I want things to go my way.

This means there are situations when my ability to
surrender proves more challenging. For instance, my friends
deciding against the restaurant I prefer or surrendering
while arguing. But as hard as it might feel, surrendering
is a goldmine of emotional information, so it's worth
practicing. Besides, wrestling our lives into submission
doesn't guarantee we'll get what we want.

5. Hope

*Hope is a resurrection to be
carried in your heart always.*

Hope is your guiding star. Hope must remain no matter what the day brings: tragedy or goodness. When one loses hope based on experience, one believes in a darker force. A lowering of self and others to a place where hope can never live.

Humans are survivors. Therefore, no human wants to live in a cave of darkness where hope cannot get in . . . a place where life does not exist.

You can hide there. But you cannot live there.

A life without hope is no life. When all hope goes, all life goes, too. And so, you see how losing hope is not an option.

Hope is your savior, your way out of the dark.

You can rely on hope because only hope keeps you in your life's light and holds the light for others.

Hope is a light that brings you more hope.

Hope is not a false claim. It is the act of saying yes to life. That is hope. So, say yes. Life is what you have, so we ask that you remain hopeful and live a life steeped in light.

Being laid up in bed wasn't a new experience for me. From ages nine to twelve, I endured frequent hospitalizations and surgeries that sometimes kept me flat on my back for months.

Back then, when I couldn't do something for myself, my requests for help were often ignored by nurses who had neither the time nor patience to cater to my needs. My parents juggled full-time jobs. They visited me in the hospital in Manhattan when they could while providing for my siblings at home in the Bronx. Overwhelmed by their suffering left little room to care for mine adequately. I learned at an early age how to fend for myself.

Self-reliance was a survival mechanism as a child, but it seamlessly morphed into stubborn independence as an adult. I became reluctant to ask others for help because the thought twisted my stomach into anxious knots. I faced this predicament again, in my midforties, after a hysterectomy.

I lived alone. The pain became unbearable on that first morning back home from the hospital. I couldn't get out of bed. How was I going to feed myself or get to the bathroom?

The idea that I should rely on someone brought familiar turmoil. Caught between the needed help and my inability to ask left me emotionally paralyzed.

I felt hopeless. I descended into what appeared to be a dark hole, the bleak space I had always imagined, like the ocean's depths—frigid, black, and unwelcoming without sunlight.

I had neither anchor nor rope to keep me from drowning in sheer terror. I wrapped my comforter around me tighter and drew in a spontaneous breath of such force that my lungs filled as if blasted by a powerful air compressor.

I saw my chest cavity rise. The shock brought me back to the surface. I felt the soft sheets beneath me.

I noticed the sun's brilliance for the first time that morning coming through the windows, bouncing light around the white walls like mirrors. I felt warmer. I pushed my comforter down to my waist.

Hope had returned. I lay there contemplating the simple truth of my situation, resolved to do the one thing I needed but had been unwilling to do moments before. I picked up the phone and called my friend. Without hesitating, she said she would be right over. I felt another surge of hope as I accepted her loving care. She hadn't denied me.

When hope left my world that morning, plummeting to an unfamiliar place of desolation startled me. On more than one occasion, that devastating time has kept me snuggled to hope whenever I feel it slipping away. I've seen the alternative, and that hole of hell is no place I want to revisit.

Reflections

Hope is important for those who have chartered a path of spirit, light, and love. So, it is important to maintain a relationship with hope. These questions are designed to help you discover hope's role in your life.

1. What does hope mean to you?
2. How does feeling hopeful influence your life?
3. Have there been circumstances in your life that have made you lose hope? If so, did hope return? How did you regain hope?

What I have come to understand about hope is that being optimistic doesn't mean

I deny my troubles, as in "Don't worry, be happy." Feeling hopeful is the only way I can live with my troubles. Hope keeps us resilient and flexible, no matter what comes our way.

6. Letting Go

You can only let go of what you have wholeheartedly embraced.

Your life is a whole life, made of this and that. Therefore, the totality of your being is affected when you hold on to anything that hides a better course. An inability to let go harms the one holding on, which can feel like making a fist. How tightly you clench your fist determines the amount of pain holding on creates.

Can you feel the pain of your clenched fist refusing to let go? If you do, is it not then wise to release the pain?

Notice what you hold.

Notice how it makes you feel.

Notice with calm and compassion if it is hurting you.

Why would you want to hurt self when you can love self even more? Therefore, more than any other practice, one must look at what makes release feel impossible, for then one can determine if letting go offers a brighter path.

Not allowing the self to let go means fear is the motivator; fear has won. But fear can take life away from you, and if you don't let go, you cannot see the other side or what is next. Fear can close all doors to what you want.

Letting go can open doors.

Letting go means you experience the expansive nature of ease so you can progress forward, releasing yourself into the new, change, and freedom.

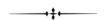

My seven-year relationship with Lindsey ended when she told me she was in love with someone else. Letting go of her and our future, our plans, the entire life I had built around our time together felt like jumping without a parachute. I had no clue how to land safely without her. I wasn't ready to take the leap, and accept I would be on my own.

I was so unwilling to let go that I remained living in our home while she left me alone most nights to meet her new lover. Even after I moved out, I couldn't let go of her promise of a lasting relationship. I stayed in the crisis of that betrayal far longer than I should have allowed.

When I think about this situation, the nausea in my stomach returns, as I recall once again how much pain I put myself through and how long I obsessed about her. I spent years reigniting the hurt and disappointment that wouldn't allow me to move on.

Reflecting on that cringeworthy time, I see how holding onto Lindsey meant my life was tethered to hers. I was only living half a life.

While she and I were still a couple, I had given a Tarot Guidance reading to a woman who wanted to adopt a child. Rose had left a lucrative career to do all of what was necessary to be ready when the adoption agency called. Unfortunately, time went by with disappointing results. She and her husband were still waiting for that phone call a year later.

Rose asked whether she should continue to put her career on hold for the sake of the adoption or get back to work. There was no question that she and her husband would keep their names on the list of prospective parents, but Guidance advised her to let go of the focus this took. They told her that returning to her career would alleviate stress because the waiting, the wanting, and the tight hold on this single-focused plan caused her to suffer.

A few weeks after her reading, Rose called me. She had come home from shopping for new work clothes to a phone message from the adoption agency on her answering machine (a time before we all carried cell phones). There was a baby who needed a family.

Not everyone will obtain the immediate miraculous effects of letting go as my client did, but her experience speaks volumes to the truth in the saying "When one door closes, another opens." Sometimes to move ahead, we must find the courage to close the door.

When I finally closed the door on any thought that I would once again be intimate with Lindsey, I felt the ease Guidance talked about and had an experience that like my client, came unexpectedly. I realized that, like Lindsey, I was also unhappy in our relationship and that her leaving turned out to be the best thing for me.

It's not uncommon for a positive turn of events to catch me by surprise when I let go. Like the time I lost a small gold earring with a garnet at its center.

Years earlier, I had ordered the pair specifically made to my taste because garnet is my birthstone. When I lost one of the earrings, I fretted about where it could be. Finally, after a frustrating, exhaustive three-day search with no results, I felt ready to move on. There was nothing more I could do about the situation. I made peace with letting the earring go.

A few days later, while looking through my jewelry drawer, I picked up a solid gold pin with a hollow back. As I turned it over, I found my earring wedged deeply inside.

The lesson of letting go reminds me of the song Doris Day sang in the Hitchcock movie *The Man Who Knew Too Much*. "Que Será, Será"—what will be will be.

I've thought about what letting go offers. When I melt into "what will be will be," I release whatever hold I imagine I have. Letting go allows the chips to fall where they will. This allows me to see people for who they truly are and not who I want them to be. Letting go allows events to unfold as they will, enabling me to trust more in the Universe's expansive nature. Letting go makes room for what's possible.

Reflections

We like to be connected to family, community, and security. This is what we know, so "letting go" can be a hard concept to comprehend as it goes against attachment, which feels more natural to us.

Attachments are fine, but not if what we're clinging to undermines our spirit, our happiness, or our sanity. If we are attached at a cost to ourselves, our own power, and our sense of place in the world, and if we are suffering through this attachment, we owe it to ourselves to feel what Guidance describes as our "clenched fist." In so doing, we may find the courage to let go.

1. Is there something you might let go of in order to feel more at ease?
2. If you've ever let go of a relationship, what has been your experience, both positive and negative?
3. What changes when you let go? What shifts? Any unexpected "gifts"? Any downsides?

What became apparent when I learned about letting go was how holding on can offer a sense of security. But feeling safe, by believing in the assuredness of what we're holding, often masks how scary it is to head into the unknown. Letting go can release that fearful tension.

When we let go with conviction, with a sense that we are doing right by ourselves, at that junction, we might be in the dark about what's next, but by honoring what's better for us, we are affirming the deep care we have for ourselves. This act of love makes room for better uplifting opportunities to present themselves. Experiences we wouldn't have had by holding on.

7. Jealousy

Jealousy is the best way to discover what it is you want.

Jealousy creates a bitter taste that feeds on toxins you cannot afford to digest. But with awareness, jealousy enlightens you to what you want.

With awareness, jealousy calls in what is your best dream or your best self, and in this, jealousy can no longer bother you.

Jealousy then becomes a motivator to greater things.

It is simple. When you become jealous, all you must do is ask what you are jealous of.

Look at what feeds your jealousy, for this is the gift of knowing what you want. Look with both eyes open to decide whether you will reach for it . . . whether you truly want what you think you do not have.

If you decide you want what you don't have, your choice is to get it—have it—find ways to embrace it, and you will be jealous no more.

If you decide not to reach for it, then we ask that you let it go with a finite goodbye, so you will never be jealous of it again.

If you are wise to jealousy, it offers you a choice and can feed your soul.

The wanting, the desire, the responsibility to have or to have not is jealousy's lesson. What you choose is up to you. Embrace what you want or release its hold. Either way, jealousy's impact on your life will hurt you no more.

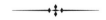

I developed scoliosis (curvature of the spine) at age twelve. At thirty-eight, my orthopedic surgeon determined that the S-shaped twist in my spine had become worse. The window to correct the pressure on my lungs and heart was closing fast.

I remained on the operating table for more than ten hours. My torso had rotated so far to the right that the surgeon had to attach two titanium rods and cut out three ribs to straighten me upright.

The painful recovery meant long hours lying in bed while staring at the ceiling. This gave me plenty of time to think about what my life would be like when I was fully capable of having a life again.

Music had always been important to me. I have young memories of spending time with my dad listening to his albums on the stereo. While he sat on the couch with his eyes closed, I sat alongside him taking in what we heard. I envisioned a battlefield with every blast of cannon fire during Tchaikovsky's "1812 Overture." I smiled while Erroll Garner's feather-like fingers flew over the piano keys and I sang along to every number from *West Side Story*, an accomplishment I can still repeat today.

At age six, my parents bought a used, weary upright piano, a massive piece of furniture with many of the ivories missing.

I started taking lessons right away. Playing the piano felt natural as if music had been trapped inside me, finally freed to express itself.

I went through my assignments at rapid speed. I excelled. I felt a kinship with the piano, and for the first time, I connected with an activity that was truly my own. I fell in love. But my blossoming relationship with the instrument was short-lived.

Three years after starting lessons, I went into the hospital. This initial surgery to correct the congenital difference in the length of my legs, began a four-year cycle of many more surgeries and time spent in the children's ward at the Hospital for Special Surgery in Manhattan, away from the Bronx and away from the piano.

I didn't resume lessons until junior high school. I enjoyed playing as I had before and made enough progress to gain admittance into New York's High School of Music and Art, but my connection with the piano had become strained. By the time I entered college, I wanted to major in music but felt incapable of pursuing that goal.

Instead of becoming the professional musician I fantasized about, I grew obsessively envious of others who made that choice. When I attended live music shows, my jealousy surfaced like an overindulgent child I couldn't quiet. I wanted to be on stage too. My moodiness made me a critical listener.

During my recovery from back surgery, I thought about this annoying, lifelong, unresolved relationship with music-making, and that's when Guidance's words came through.

Pursue what you are jealous of or let it go.

I imagined music fading away, only to discover I was grief-stricken. Giving up music wasn't an option, so I took Guidance's advice.

With my back finally healed, I enrolled at a local community college to give music its due. My decision to obtain the music degree I wanted would offer the professional status I craved but had denied for too long.

By then, I played conga drums. I hadn't touched a piano in years, so I enrolled as a percussionist. I took the required classes in sight singing and theory and learned three new instruments: timpani, snare drum, and classical marimba. At the end of the year, I would have to play those instruments in front of the music faculty, who would decide if my dream to become a bona-fide music major was in the cards.

When I wasn't at my day job, I attended classes and scribed my name on one of the school's practice room doors. I spent evening hours and long weekends there learning the instruments and the music my private percussion teacher assigned.

During that period, I dealt with a tremendous amount of self-doubt about my ability to pull off what my professors required. I also missed my dog, who wound up in the care of friends to make sure she didn't miss a walk or a feeding. I carried those weighty issues around most of the time except when I entered the stillness of one of the sound-proof practice cubicles. There, I felt as if I had been sprinkled with fairy dust.

Like Cinderella at the ball, I felt included. I belonged with these people I once envied. I liked fitting in.

After nine months of classes, the time came to jury. I played all three instruments, then waited in the hall while the three professors deliberated.

I felt queasy. I had mixed feelings about hearing their critiques, especially how I had or hadn't tuned the timpani correctly.

It didn't take long for them to call me back. I stared into their faces, trying to get a fix on what they thought. My percussion teacher broke the silence. I made the cut.

Although I can't physically skip, my joy felt like I did. I left their company elated by their acceptance.

Two weeks later, I found myself questioning whether I wanted to commit the next two years to a classical music degree. Why would I give up the one opportunity I had craved for so long? My misgivings puzzled me, which fostered my curiosity. A memory of an incident in junior high school came into focus.

I was seated in the front row of a typing class when Mr. Gardner, the music director, entered, asking for volunteers to join his orchestra. To stabilize my curved back, which looked like a corkscrew by then—I wore a clunky, oversized brace that covered my torso from hip to neck. Three steel rods—two in the back and one in front—protruded so far outward it looked like I was wearing a barrel.

My chin rested on a wide oversized metal platform covered in tan leather. The brace was heavy, and I moved like Frankenstein, with my head and mid-section rigid. Nothing I wore—no item of clothing—could hide the contraption.

Wearing a back brace was embarrassing enough, and

walking around with a visible limp didn't help. The surgery to correct the leg-length discrepancy failed, leaving me with limited movement of my knee and foot, plus I still wore a significant lift on my left shoe as I had before the surgery.

When Mr. Gardner made his request, I wanted to wave my hand above my head, so he'd notice me. My excitement to play in his orchestra had me nearly jumping out of my seat.

But during the seconds between his announcement and my desire, I had a vision of gimping across the stage in the school's auditorium, wearing the required crisp white button-down shirt stretched to the max around my barrel-braced chest. I stood out, a deformed figure with all eyes on me. Humiliated, I remained frozen in my chair and watched five other twelve-year-olds leave the room with Mr. Gardner.

I hadn't understood until that memory resurfaced, how those years in and out of the hospital, away from my peers, left me feeling years behind them. I felt incapable of catching up to their progress, both socially and musically. My defeat ran deep.

As I gnawed away at those reflections, I realized how, after I returned to playing the piano, the initial confidence that carried me, in the beginning, was replaced by self-doubt as solid as stone. The more I felt I didn't measure up, the more jealous I became.

Music turned into a jealous vehicle when I watched others excel because I believed so little in myself. My adult life was being run by a child. That child was me, still sitting in typing class, feeling inferior witnessing normal-looking kids raise their hands to pursue what they wanted while I remained on the sidelines.

I allowed my dreams to disappear. But the validation in my musical abilities shown by the music professors helped me to understand that it was I who held myself back because I didn't value myself.

I carried the oppressive weight of wanting to belong while denying myself access due to how I looked. Being accepted by those professors challenged my perceptions, healing the many years I felt unworthy.

Guidance predicted that once I followed where jealousy led, I would find resolution. And I did.

Jealousy had locked me into a self-destructive cycle that chipped away at my self-esteem. I understood this now and realized that my focus on becoming a professional musician was an old dream that I no longer needed or wanted. I called the head of the music department to decline his offer to attend school in the fall.

Back surgery had freed me from the ill effects of my twisted spine, but the insight and clarity I gained during those nine months at the community college freed me from the jealousy I carried toward those who chose music as their career.

I figured this would be the end of the story, but another door swung open.

In early August, shortly after deciding to forgo the music degree, I received a call from a Venezuelan guitar player and singer-songwriter looking for a local percussionist to accompany her. Two weeks later, she hired me to play the conga drums onstage at an outdoor music festival in Jacksonville, Oregon.

I spent the next two years touring with Irene. She paid me to play at small and large venues such as the Vancouver Folk Festival, sometimes as a duo and other times with a drum set player and bassist.

That experience led to opening a hand-drum school where, for the next ten years, I taught children and adults. I also published an instructional hand-drum book with a DVD that showcased my curriculum.

The irony has never been lost on me that once I let go of my ambition to be a professional musician, I became one.

I chose to understand jealousy's impact on my life only to experience Guidance's point again—that a shift in awareness can alter a life for the better. Healing jealousy brought rewards that, like my back surgery, reshaped my very existence.

Reflections

Jealousy is your road map. If you allow it to speak to you, it will clarify how you would like to travel.

1. What effect does jealousy have on you and the quality of your life?
2. Can you identify any recurring themes, situations, or types of people that illicit a jealous feeling?
3. What might you gain by pursuing or releasing what you are jealous of?

Facing my demons means facing those traits I'm less proud of. And I'm not proud that I spent years resenting musicians whose talents deserved my applause.

Thanks to Guidance's counsel, I grew to understand how jealousy festered because I diminished myself. These days, I'm hard-pressed to think of any situation where jealousy makes me feel good about myself or evokes generosity toward others. Does this ring true for you too?

8. Gratitude

Gratitude is an unseen force that heals. It helps.

To reach for gratitude, all one must do is to remember to be thankful. When one is grateful, one's heart opens to the bounty of what life is. For your life matters as all life matters. Being grateful reminds you.

No one is alone on this earth. Gratitude connects you to the Divine and to others, a memory of connectedness that opens hearts and feeds your soul.

Gratitude has no boundary. It's limitless. Saying thank you is pure of self, pure of ego, pure of desire. Gratitude pulls you out of self . . . pulls you away from the poor-me stance that would have you believe you are a victim.

Gratitude is your blessing.

Your improvement.

Your ability to know more, to see farther to direct change.

Be thankful. For gratitude lifts your spirit. Gratitude praises life, the life that is yours, the one you know. Make time to be grateful, and you will feel more of what living offers.

I don't recall when gratitude journals became the rage or when I heard about them or from whom, but I found the idea worthy. Back then, I was troubled by my inability to get close to people. I felt emotionally distant from those I cared about, unable to connect fully.

I spent many years admonishing myself for feeling this vast separation from others. So, when I heard how a gratitude journal might open my closed heart, I jumped at the idea.

At bedtime, I picked up a pen and opened my black, hardbound journal, with its unlined paper, to write what I felt grateful for. My dog ended up on the page along with my home, friends, job, and a few other things. I scrawled a rather comprehensive list, but no matter how many nights I put pen to paper, the exercise fell flat.

I might have been writing my grocery list. I couldn't muster an emotional connection. After a few frustrating weeks, I put the journal back in its drawer, convinced that although gratitude might work for some, the practice clearly didn't work for me.

As I matured and grew in awareness, my inability to give freely to others became increasingly troubling. Holding back emotionally from friends and lovers while seeking their reassurances before I would show affection, struck me as selfish and self-absorbed.

I was sick of the constraints I put on myself. Would a practice of gratitude change this view?

For inspiration, I went back to what Guidance said on the subject. When I read the passage about gratitude pulling focus away from the self, I probably lifted my head from the page because at that moment, I noticed a photo on my desk with fresh eyes.

The picture shows my friend Ann in the foreground with her back to the viewer. She is looking up at white, billowy clouds in the distance, circling like halos that hover above the mountain peaks of Ama Dablam in the eastern Himalayan range.

With her arms raised high above her head, Ann reaches into the vastness of a purplish-gray wintry sky. Her fingertips are spread, stretched wide, pointing upward into the atmosphere.

After months of staring at this image, I recognized a reverence I hadn't seen before. It was as if Ann were praying, thanking the heavens for her good fortune—to be alone there, amid nature, surrounded by the overwhelming beauty of snowy mountains as far as the eye could see.

With the sun gleaming through my office windows, I stood from my chair and raised my arms above my head, copying Ann's pose. I said *thank you* out loud to no one and "no-thing" in particular.

I bolstered my hope. I waited. The exercise returned zero results. Like the gratitude journal before, I felt detached from my mission. What was I supposed to feel when I gave thanks?

Unlike last time, I refused to give up. I remained motivated. I committed to the practice. Each day upon entering my office, I reached out to the Universe, raising my arms to say thank you.

Again, I was confronted by the familiar protective layer around my heart. With my eyes closed, I asked questions. Where is gratitude? Is it in my heart? Is gratitude all around me?

The saying "fake it till you make it" might explain what happened. After weeks of simply raising my arms to say thank you, a type of miracle occurred.

My mind went blank. My questions about gratitude slipped away. A warm sense settled through me, the way a smooth shot of whiskey soothes.

A vision appeared. I saw a large slate gray metal cage wrapped around my heart. As I watched, the door flung open. Then the entire cumbersome contraption vanished.

Stunned, I observed my heart, revealed for the first time—crimson, large, and bright—beating exposed and free. I wondered if the cage would return. It didn't. I expected to feel vulnerable with a heart so unprotected. But that didn't happen either.

My heart continued to pump. Its new healthy status in my chest felt natural—more natural than the safety I had wrapped it in for far longer.

The image of Dickens's Ebenezer Scrooge came into view. I had never read the book, *A Christmas Carol*, but had seen countless movie versions, and each had been fixed in my imagination since childhood.

Three ghosts visit Scrooge on Christmas Eve after he falls asleep. One, in particular, takes him back to his childhood that is filled with hardship and disappointment. The sad memories transform his heart from one of bitterness to love and compassion. Like Scrooge, I also remembered why I had closed my heart in the first place.

I learned at an early age that an open, expecting, vulnerable heart gets hurt. As a child, I experienced disappointment from doctors and my parents, who all promised I would be better off after surgery to equalize my leg lengths. The trauma of that surgery and other failed surgical attempts left scars, not only on the operated leg but on my young loving heart.

That heart—the one I came into this world with, the one with all its caring purpose—was battered and bruised. I protected her.

Although I know of people who became more loving when they were denied love as a child, I became cautious, unable to trust that others had my best interests at heart. This left me cynical and emotionally distant, not just from others but from myself as well.

I spent years unable to greet friends with a smile instead of a wary eye. My gratitude practice, like Scrooge's ghosts, changed my view.

Gratitude is a memory of connectedness that opens hearts and feeds your soul.

Guidance's words ring true for me. When I say "thank you," and I do it quite often these days, my heart softens and once again I allow gratitude's oceanic power of unconditional love to wash over me.

Reflections

I went from being someone who couldn't figure out what gratitude could do for me to someone whose spiritual well-being increased due to the practice. And wouldn't you know—when I feel grateful, my gratitude compounds.

Gratitude offers us a moment to feel one with love. With that said, there are as many ways to practice gratitude as there are ideas. So, whether you already say "thanks" or are struggling as I did, finding what works is important. Here are some suggestions.

1. Would holding a rock in your hand while saying what you're grateful for keep gratitude close? And if so, why not keep that rock in your pocket or handbag throughout the day to stay humble to all that gratitude offers you.
2. Would writing or reciting a gratitude prayer before going to bed at night or before getting out of bed in the morning aid your practice of gratitude?
3. Would raising your arms up in the air to say "thank you," like I did, be helpful? I continue to love this ritual.

I often buy books that end up on my shelf without being read. I need to remember that I own them. Years later, I'll come upon one of these books collecting dust and open its pages to discover that it's the perfect read, exactly what I needed in the moment.

Like those books, I shelved gratitude for years until the timing proved exactly right. Trust the timing that's right for you. A grateful practice can be done hourly, daily, weekly, or whenever you remember.

There's no right or wrong method either, just the one that's right for you. My only hope is that you add gratitude to your spiritual practice because, as I discovered, the benefits will show themselves to you.

9. Money

Money is a partnership. This exchange of money for service is a good exchange.

Money is not a value. It is not evil, nor is it kind. The energy of money was not meant to be judged.

Money is in your world to create. To enable. Money is a creative tool.

Choose money as your tool if you decide that money would help you as any tool would.

Ask for this tool, for money can come. It comes as you need it.

Mold money—like art, like clay.

Mold it and create with it. Keep your sights on what money offers. Decide how this tool will help you and what it is you can create with it.

Freedom is not created from money. Freedom is a state of being. What you do with money can remind you of freedom, but money does not make you free. Nothing can set you free in this world but you.

Money is not about deservedness. Some have more because they stretch their arms toward it. Their feeling of limitlessness brings more. Money is just one symbol of what limitlessness can feel like.

All is infinite. Humans cannot grasp this. But finiteness is what humans grasp and so believe that money too is finite.

Humans grasp limitations because limits are all around them. Humans see that the body is limited, a contained vessel, so they believe that all is finite through this view. But seeing with eyes is only one way to see—it is not the whole picture.

Take in the beauty of your body but look to your heart, for you will see what is true. Look to your gut, for the gut of knowingness is that there are no limitations. Money, too, has no limits.

Yet money is no more valuable than what one does with it. Its power resides in how one uses it. In and of itself, money sits and waits without value.

Do not allow money to claim your view of the world or of self. Know rightly that money exists like everything in your world. How it exists, in small or large measure, is up to you.

Money was tight in my family. To combat this ongoing issue, my mom squirreled away cash in white envelopes. I must have been eleven when I discovered her system for budgeting hidden in her underwear drawer.

Each envelope was marked in my mom's neat cursive penmanship. Tucked away were envelopes for food, clothes, the mortgage, the gas bill, etc. She explained how she divvied up every paycheck she and my dad brought home to ensure she could pay for the things we needed along with her priorities.

One of my mom's priorities was to get us away from the oppressive heat of the Bronx every summer. While other kids on our block stood in line ordering ice cream from the Mr. Softee truck, my mom said no when I asked.

She argued that one more quarter in an envelope meant swimming in a pool at a bungalow colony in upstate New York while families across the street fanned themselves on their front porches all summer.

I'm grateful for my mom's realistic lessons about money, but her openness scarred me in a way. The carryover from a childhood in which the lack of money was always an issue between my parents instilled my belief that money came in a limited, finite supply. My interpretation was that no matter how many envelopes were bursting with green, there would never be enough for life's fun extras, like a vanilla soft serve with chocolate sprinkles.

In my midthirties, my priority was to purchase a home, but it meant having a roommate to help pay the bills. I lived on a shoestring, from paycheck to paycheck, and amassed credit card debt that I obsessed about. My inability to pay off the cards screwed with my self-esteem.

I believed that money naturally gravitated to some people, while my ability to access this powerful tool was as elusive as touching a cloud. I was convinced that, compared to others, I would always be the poor relation.

To alleviate my stress, I sought advice from my mentor, Claudia Leone, a wonderful psychic and spiritual wise woman. Claudia told me that money showed up anytime, from anywhere, even when least expected.

She offered a pragmatic example. She hoped this would expand my view. If I believed that money could only be accumulated through savings, then this limited the way money could come to me.

Claudia's words reminded me of an experience I had years earlier when I lacked the money to cover my property taxes. A few weeks before the due date, I opened my mailbox to find a card from my mother with a check for two thousand dollars. This amount was slightly more than I owed the county.

Mom lived on Social Security and a small retirement pension from her bookkeeping job. I knew her to be a generous person, but her usual gifts came on my birthday and amounted to twenty-five or sometimes one hundred dollars. I never expected a check coming from my mom for such a large amount for no discernible reason.

I called her and found out that she had sold her diamond engagement ring, which had no sentimental value since divorcing my dad. She wanted my sister, brother, and me to share in the profits.

As I remembered this, I had tangible proof that money entered my life in surprising, unplanned ways. Yet I continued to view money through a limited lens, which affected my mood. When flush with cash, I had no complaints. If I couldn't afford to buy a cup of coffee, this bummed me out.

My emotional relationship with money was a daily roller-coaster ride, with highs and lows. Exhausting. Guidance sent a message that hit me over the head,

Don't let money claim your mood.

Their words were as loud as the alarm clock beside my bed. I woke up.

It was true that money controlled my emotional barometer. I allowed this. I not only remained a victim to my past and how I grew up, but I was a victim every day. I felt mortified.

From being fearful about not having enough to obsessing about wanting more, all my thoughts were focused on lack. The all-consuming internal dialogue about money always had a negative spin.

Yet I owned a home. I had food on the table. I made ends meet. I got by. I supported myself. I had been clever. I rented a room in my house to help with bills. At each moment, I was okay and better off than many.

I needed to change my relationship with money. Rather than complaining about the lack of it, I thought about what money might offer. I fantasized about taking my sister to an exotic beach location, paying for a girlfriend's meal at a fancy restaurant, or donating thousands of dollars to a good cause.

This last thought tapped my frustration the way it did every time I sent a lesser dollar amount than I wanted to a worthy organization. Wouldn't it feel better to write checks for larger amounts? I vowed that next time, no matter how little my donation, I would mail it without the "poor me" attitude that had become my usual habit.

I widened my perspective to include a more positive spin. Perhaps one similar to my mom when she added one more dollar to the Bungalow Colony envelope, knowing she would spend her days lounging poolside while nights would be at a mahjong table gabbing with girlfriends.

My new relationship with money worked to ease the tension, but it would take more soul-searching to heal my long-held belief that I didn't deserve money. To do this, I unearthed old messages about money that came not only from my parents but also from close relatives and the world at large.

No matter the memory, I swallowed how not having enough money meant I wasn't as "good" as other people. Therefore, not as worthy as other people. I gave money way too much power. Not only did money affect my happiness, but it added to the list of ways I ridiculed myself. That needed to stop.

Motivated, I developed an internal alarm system that has remained. When I judge my life based on the dollars in my bank account, I swipe all the negative thoughts aside before they have a chance to calcify into my brain.

Guidance's simple message continues to be a game-changer. I refuse to let money, whether it comes in large amounts or small, claim my mood.

I kept money and myself in a confined space because of my small, confined ideas, but I have no desire to put money or myself back in that box. The values I place on money are mine, created through my own understanding, so I get to decide on money's diminishing or enhancing returns. The changes I made in my outlook richly improved my life, adding worth that no amount of money could ever buy.

Reflections

Most of us no longer use the barter system. We use money as our method of exchange for goods and services. This means most people in the world think about money.

Simply put, money affects us. Whether you have a healthy or unhealthy relationship with it, questioning money's role in your life and its influence is a worthy undertaking.

1. Do you believe your relationship with money is healthy or unhealthy? And if it is unhealthy, what would enable you to heal?
2. Are there specific beliefs you have about money that you would like to change?
3. How does your relationship with money affect your mood?

When I explored my views about money, I realized I had an unhealthy relationship with it. I knew then that money and I would have to come to some understanding if we were to play nice together.

Money had a negative effect on me. This might be different for you. Yet, no matter how you view money's influence in your life, what's important is to be free of money's controlling grasp. And to do this, it makes sense to decide who is in control.

10. Intuition

Follow what you know, and what you know will guide your path.

THE HIGH PRIESTESS

You hold the keys to what it is you are seeking. No one knows better than you, but you must learn to access this. Going against what you know is your decision, but a wiser decision is to follow.

Your intuitive knowledge is your sixth sense.

Intuition lives in the deep recesses of your body, and this knowing will guide you in the moment.

This knowing will set your life free to follow what is meant to be.

How does one know what is true for them? Do you feel exalted? Does your body feel elevated to a place of deep recognition? Do you feel love pulsing through you? At that moment, you may not have all the answers. But it will feel as if you are soaring, open, as if the waters have parted, and the birds have sung to you.

Not listening to your truth will feel like going against self and that is when the self-doubt can start.

Fear may come as you attempt to further and follow this Truth path, this Truth day, this Truth moment, this Truth voice. But fear is often a way of saying no, and when you say "no" to your truth, your denial feels constricted in body and soul.

What is there to fear about what your deep knowing tells you?

We ask that you sit quietly. Listen to what your Truth is. For it is in the quiet moments that one can hear what is meant to be when one is open to listening.

We ask only that, in your life, you trust that feeling of expansion—you trust your knowing. For that is your truth. *That is what doing for self is. And in doing for self, you will know and do what's best.*

M y work life has been varied. I've stood behind counters wrapping Burger King Whoppers, and I've made lattes for morning commuters at a local coffee shop. I've been a recreation therapist, administrative aide, telephone operator, director of a nonprofit, and a retail salesperson. I could add to this list, but regardless of where I worked, the longest I ever stayed at one job was seven years—hence, my long resume.

Around my fortieth birthday, I quit another job, my first with good benefits and a retirement plan. I told everyone, even those who thought I had lost my mind, that I wanted to "live the life of an artist." I had no idea what that meant. What I did know was that I had grown tired of the nine-to-five routine. I cut myself loose. Once again, I contemplated my next move.

On a bright sunny autumn afternoon, I put a leash on Bow, my black border collie, to take her on a walk. We had gone about a block when I saw a "For Rent" sign in the window of a small vacant house. The dwelling's footprint was tiny, more like a one-car garage, but it had the bones of a cute bungalow.

As I stared at the welcoming covered front porch, I was overcome by a deep knowing to make that little house mine. It was an absurd idea. I had a mortgage to pay, and without steady work, money was tight.

To make ends meet, I rented a room in my home and offered hand-drum lessons in my basement, but my appointment calendar was never full. How about adding one more expense? I pushed the strong yearning aside. Logic won. I continued my walk.

The next afternoon, Bow and I passed the rental sign again.

The pang to inquire about the space returned, along with an uplift of excitement that I recognized.

My intuition exerted itself again, locking me into a decision I seemed to lack any control over. I had no idea why this house wanted me, but I jotted down the phone number.

The landlord answered on the second ring. When he asked what I would be doing with the space, without hesitation, I said a hand-drum school. I spoke with confidence as if I knew about this plan all along, which I did not. The landlord said he would think about it and call with his decision.

That night, I couldn't sleep. The little house didn't come cheap. My thoughts ricocheted between hoping I had won the owner's approval and hoping my request would be denied so I could avoid financial ruin.

The next day, I heard back. The house was mine. At forty years old, with no business savvy, commercial experience, or proof of financial solvency, the landlord chose me over an insurance company with a viable business plan. I figured it was meant to be.

I grabbed a legal pad. Sitting at my kitchen table, I wrote a mission statement for a hand-drum school, feeling giddy as if I had won the lottery instead of someone who had no idea how she would pay for such a crazy notion.

Ideas flowed without effort, swept along by an undeniable passion for a school I didn't know I wanted until the day before.

When I put my pen down, what lay before me were descriptions of classes, the times I would be teaching, and a pricing plan that would hopefully earn income. At the top of my notes, I scrawled a name for the business: Hands-on Rhythm and Drum School. The quick ease with which the title surfaced surprised me. I'm terrible at naming things. I hemmed and hawed for two weeks, wondering what to call my dog until a friend finally suggested the name Bow. Yet, like everything else having to do with this school, all the pieces seemed to come together effortlessly.

I ran that hand-drum school for ten years. It attracted a large loyal following of wonderful people. Many became friends, and the school grew in ways far beyond what I envisioned that afternoon at my kitchen table.

I not only gave lessons and brought other drummers in to teach, but I also lugged hand drums into the community to work with hundreds of organizations and schools.

My degree in Therapeutic Recreation also came in handy. I brought drums to marginalized populations, such as incarcerated men, developmentally disabled adults, and women recovering from drug addiction, to name a few. I also produced a well-respected community drum festival, and national and local conferences invited me to speak about the health and wellness aspects of hand drumming.

Hands-on Rhythm and Drum School was hard work. There were days when I felt overwhelmed and months when I worried I might not have the rent money. But the school fostered a confidence I never knew and brought gifts beyond my wildest imagination—like becoming a sponsored artist for Toca Percussion, one of the largest drum manufacturers in the world.

I also developed a unique hand-drum curriculum. Despite concerns about my writing skills and lack of a music degree, I signed with a well-known publisher, who turned my teaching method into an instructional book with an accompanying DVD.

On the afternoon that Bow and I stood outside the little bungalow that begged me to rent it, I pushed my fears aside. I had the gumption to say "yes."

Unbeknownst to me at the time, saying "yes" aligned with my declaration to live the life of an artist. By running a drum school, I learned that being an artist means following one's passion. And following one's passion brings levels of fear and risk.

Looking back, it seemed as if my decision to rent the bungalow came from every part of me. As if my mind, heart, body, and higher self were connected, creating a strong partnership that signaled the pure rightness of my intentions.

I didn't have all the answers, but that didn't seem to matter. I trusted my intuition—the deeper knowing, a *truth* that signaled excitement, expanded my awareness, and brought a sense of comfort as if I were being beckoned back home to a hearth familiar and inviting.

Reflections

We are all born with intuitive knowing. We already have this skill, so it's not about finding it. It's about believing in it again and trusting ourselves enough to listen.

Using our sixth sense means we're able to identify that surge of "rightness" and expansiveness when it begs our attention. Conversely, when we don't listen, we often feel off-kilter.

When it comes to our intuition, gaining confidence is a key component. Take time with the questions to explore your relationship with your own knowing.

1. We've all experienced that jolt to call a friend. I've been known to dismiss these opportunities, but noting what happens, whether the call is made or not, helps to build intuitive confidence. What do you notice when you dismiss or follow through on your intuition?
2. Our intuition strengthens when we receive validation. What has been your response to this nod, whether it comes from a person, an oracle card, a Tarot deck, or any other source? How do you react?

Many women, including myself, have been told to listen to our intuition when we walk down a dark street alone at night. We are also warned to follow our instincts on a first date to pay attention to those "red flags."

Why, then, wouldn't we give intuition its respectful due all the time?

Building our intuitive skill is a muscle we need to flex and use continually. The foundational key that allows our intuition to gain strength is the belief in our abilities. Through practice, we gain confidence, become more discerning, and more trusting of what we hear, so we can act upon what we know more often.

11. Acceptance

Acceptance is asking you to pay attention.

Acceptance is your ability to meet what is. Denying what is true becomes your struggle. Acceptance ends resistance. Ending your resistance will relax your shoulders, help you to unclench your jaw, make you whole, for in you is the ability to see clearly what you do to self when you cannot accept.

We ask that you be ever mindful.

Acceptance opens doors to the self you seek.

Trust in the moment. Acceptance offers clarity and brings what's possible. It allows you the freedom to make wiser choices that will benefit you.

Accept what is true in you and in others, with love and compassion. Your truest choice toward change is with an accepting heart.

"I want to get to the point where I feel good about my decision to buy a new car."

Once again, my friend JoJo had to think seriously about trading in her old car for a newer model.

For the past three years, anytime JoJo drove her fifteen-year-old Mazda to her mechanic, and that was often, she wanted to replace the relic. This proved to be a difficult decision, and she agonized about buying brand new.

JoJo had only purchased used cars. Her parents had instilled in her their belief that buying a new car was no different from throwing money in a trash can. "New cars depreciate the moment they leave the lot," they told her.

The day after JoJo received another thousand-dollar bill for auto repairs, she became excited again about test driving the latest vehicles. She knew she needed to take the plunge, but this went against her parents' financial advice. By the time we talked, she was plagued with the same self-doubt and inner conflict that kept her from buying years earlier.

In my experience, JoJo's hesitation wasn't unusual. Inertia can set in when we are overpowered by a fear of doing something we've never done before. Old ways of thinking often hijack decisions that might be better for us. JoJo believed, as many do, that to break free from the ideas that hold us back, we must transform them before taking action.

This is undoubtedly true in certain circumstances. For example, I knew I needed to change how I handled anger before allowing myself to enter another intimate relationship. But there are other times when we don't need to wait while we work out the conflictual cogs that get in our way. Sometimes we need to accept where we're at.

This was the case with JoJo's situation. It became apparent that what stood in the way had nothing to do with her desire to buy new but about her lifetime of buying into her parents' way of thinking, which as an adult she had never questioned.

JoJo was being emotionally pulled in opposite directions that wouldn't allow for a decision. Her bubbly enthusiasm for the car model and color she wanted conflicted with her anxiety about making the purchase.

I suggested that instead of waiting to feel grounded about her decision to buy new, which could take a while, a better course might be acceptance . . . that she felt both troubled and elated about plopping down money for the car of her dreams.

After our conversation, JoJo settled into accepting her ambiguity. This not only brought her peace of mind but also a trip to the Honda dealer.

Like JoJo, I too have experienced events that create emotions at odds with each other. One such example happened while dating online.

In my early fifties, I wanted a relationship after being single for twelve years. After every first date that didn't lead to a second date—and there were plenty of those—I questioned my age, along with my viability and disability, as the reason things weren't working out. I experienced grave self-loathing.

So, although I wanted to be in a couple, my dating mojo disappeared sometimes for weeks and months while I waited to get over my disappointment. The inertia, however, didn't bring me closer to what I wanted, so I resurrected Guidance's piece about acceptance.

Acceptance allows you the freedom to make wiser choices that will benefit you.

Like the advice I gave JoJo, I stopped waiting for the day when my age and disability no longer affected me, because that day would probably never come. I accepted how self-doubt and disappointment would remain part of my dating package, like putting on lipstick before I left the house.

Acceptance brought the truth of my situation to the surface. As Guidance predicted, relief and freedom replaced internal conflict, which enabled JoJo to buy a brand-new Honda CRV and me to return to those dating apps.

Reflections

Acceptance is a form of self-admission that liberates us. One of the most profound examples: people who admit they are alcoholics. Once alcoholics have accepted their truth, they can begin to accept themselves with all their vulnerability and frailty.

With acceptance, we meet ourselves where we're at, with compassion and understanding, so change comes more organically. But, for this to happen, it requires us to pay attention.

Acceptance also allows us to see others more clearly. When we accept others as they are, we believe what they say and what they show us. It then becomes harder to make excuses for them. It becomes easier to set boundaries. It enables us to stand in our power because reality is guiding us. We are liberated as we receive the gift of authenticity.

Acceptance acts as a harbinger of our denial. It asks: How present am I willing to be? How absolutely true can I be to myself?

1. When does denial work for you? When does it work against you?
2. What might change if you accepted a situation for what it is or accepted a person for who they show you they are?
3. What might be different if you accepted the ambiguity of your disparate thoughts or feelings?

Our emotional discomforts might motivate our desire to change. But acceptance often proves to be the most valuable way to change.

12. Failure and Success

You have no choice but to fail and succeed.

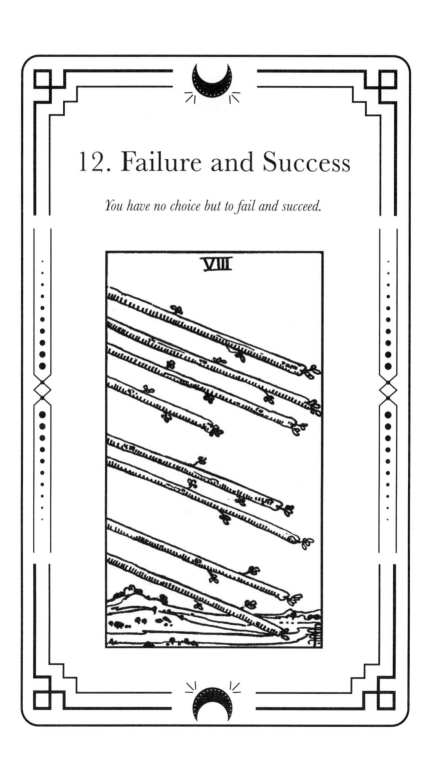

Failure and success are your badges of resiliency—proof you can survive, for both are interwoven. Success and failure bring you strength and show what you are made of.

Both inform you who you are.

Both help you to progress, continue, and grow as a person.

Success and failure feed your soul.

Failure reinforces your willingness to commit. Failure reshapes, reinvigorates, or redefines your path. Failure tempers your ego; teaches you about humility and courage; and humbles you to one of life's greatest teachings about self-acceptance.

Success breeds confidence. Success validates your path. Success glorifies all you know, what you thought, what you believed with all your heart and soul. Success reshapes, reinvigorates, or redefines your path. Success tempers your ego; teaches you about humility and courage; and humbles you to one of life's greatest teachings about self-acceptance.

Either way, success and failure clarify what you are meant to do.

All failures and successes are deemed worthy as the reality of life's ups and downs reflects the truth of your life. Failure and success are your way to understand that you're vulnerable to all that failure and success teach you, for no one is perfect.

Success and failure allow for change. They allow you to grow. In their purest form, they allow for harmony, as you learn what they want to tell you.

Do not judge success and failure measured by society's definitions. Those who only see their success and failure based on what society expects are lost to self.

Outward definitions of success will only make you feel big and import-ant. Outward definitions of failure will only make you feel small and defeated. Both, defined in this way, only skim the surface of what failure and success are.

What you do, once you fail or succeed, is up to you. But our hope is that you won't judge how failure and success enter your life.

Above all, be mindful that both success and failure are part of your legacy. Allow success and failure to bend your eye toward gratitude and you will become wise to how both are here to serve you.

When I started my hand-drum school, my main goal was to demystify the playing of congas, djembes, and other percussion instruments. I felt successful—not because I made a lot of money or because my classes were full, but because I set out to teach non-musicians how to play and enter drum circles with confidence. To that end, my students were succeeding.

During that time, I wrote an instructional hand-drum book based on the curriculum I developed. The manuscript found a publisher, and by 2008, a DVD and book set appeared on music store shelves.

From the beginning, the publisher wanted to get the prod-uct into the hands of a mainstream audience, not just in music stores. The head of sales met with a few big box stores that promised they were ready to buy. I never knew the names of those companies, but I was told they were on board.

My small project would make more money than I ever imagined. I started feeling the excitement of success pulling me forward. My ego grew with a sudden sense of importance. I pictured fame and riches.

Then, the 2008 recession hit. I was told that my hand-drum package would be replaced with guitar kits, a more popular, tried and true, less risky instrument.

Overnight, the promised success I anticipated vanished. I had been on my way up. Now I was on my way down. I felt like a failure. I became depressed, wrapped in an emotional funk I couldn't shed.

Guidance advised that I focus on my own definitions of success and failure. During this period of reflection, my thoughts returned to a meeting with the CEO of the publishing house.

While I sat on one of the grand overstuffed leather chairs in his office, he stood behind an imposing oversized wood desk with ornate carvings. He lined out his plans for the book launch, which included interviews and television appearances on shows like "TODAY" and others.

The mention of TV brought my nervous energy to a whole new level. The idea alone was more than I could take in. My body went rigid. My brain shut down for a minute or so. I stopped hearing him. I finagled the book deal through sheer luck without an agent. I was out of my depth and intimidated by the entire experience. I had no one to guide me as I sat in one of the largest publishing companies in New York City.

I didn't tell him about my freak-out. I wanted the success he promised, so I nodded my head, pretending I could cope, pretending his vision thrilled me, pretending I wasn't terrified.

Back then, being interviewed on TV wasn't the only reason for my emotional meltdown; it also had to do with the large sums of money the CEO anticipated (in fact, he said "millions.") I had a strange relationship with money. I wanted more, but on that day, my solid sense that I didn't deserve more surfaced with a vengeance.

I continued to deny all these misgivings. I stuffed my truth. I acted as if I could handle everything being offered without sharing my fears with anybody.

As I mulled this over, I remembered a message I received from Guidance years earlier. It had to do with unacknowledged feelings, especially our unexamined internal conflicts and how they can put our efforts at cross-purposes.

I recognized my experience with the book as being one of the truest examples of this ambivalence Guidance described. The recession certainly prevented the success I had been promised. But my inability to come to terms with my fears about money and fame, to admit what plagued me, played a role in sabotaging my success.

Once I understood this, I turned my attention away from blaming the box stores for creating my failure in order to put the focus back on me. How did I define the success and failure of this project for myself?

Immediately, my pride in completing the manuscript came back. This was the first time I had written a book. Plus, I found a publisher through my own ingenuity. This took more chutzpah than I ever thought I possessed. I remembered how successful I felt through my achievements. I also remembered that two publishers refused my proposal. Yet I believed so much in the book's message and purpose that I didn't feel like a failure when they turned me down.

Years ago, in my twenties, while in therapy, my counselor asked whether I was afraid of success or afraid of failure. I had no answer. The question remained a riddle I never solved, but I continued to ponder her question.

Today, that question no longer concerns me. Both success and failure influence me—not one more than the other. I learn things about myself from both experiences. When I base success and failure on outside influences, I lose that benefit. Plus, if I adhere to society's focus on money and recognition to define these terms, I'm left walking with shallow footing on shaky ground.

All of this is something to think about if I ever allow myself to be that vulnerable again. Guidance is right. I'm better off when I define success and failure for myself.

Reflections

I look at success and failure the way I view the positive and negative attributes of our astrological signs. Like astrological signs, we benefit and grow not by judging their aspects but by being aware of their influence.

1. How do your successes and failures impact you?
2. What are some of the influences that have contributed to how you define success and failure?
3. What have you learned from your successes and failures that have shaped who you are? Or what you believe? Or how you've lived?

Success can feel like we're heading upward toward possibility, while failure can feel like we can't get any traction. Switch these assumptions and we might see how failure might motivate us to try harder, while success might have us resting on our laurels, unmotivated to keep trying.

It's our personal perceptions that illuminate how success and failure affect our experiences.

13. Religion and God

*To find God, you must acknowledge self. For above all,
you are love, and love is always within you.*

XII

THE HANGED MAN.

God and religion are not one. Do not mistake religion for God. Remember what religion was created for. Religion was created to explain God, but in so doing, created a system of checks and balances so people would not stray far. To control, to explain these religious tenets, is not God.

Many religious teachings are designed to help one find God. Ritual and text, by their very nature, are used to bring one closer to God and explain God.

But God has no explanation.

Religion can only teach.

Humans question God and try to understand God, but in so doing, spend time away from God.

Spending time with God means one spends time with self.

When one listens to self, one listens to God, and when one listens to God, then one knows how hard it is to move against others. How hard it is to bring ill to others when so much good is wanting. How hard it is to frown when one can smile instead.

Humans make life hard. God does not make life hard; humans can do that by themselves.

God's truth is about light and joy, just as sorrow and breath are God.

Cultures can teach about God. Religions can find God. But each of you has God.

God is connected to all things and raises what is human to what is.

Love is love. And for those who sit with self, love is what surfaces. And in that, Love speaks to what God is, and love speaks to you. In its purest form, Love is felt, seen, heard, and accepted.

Only Love, then, is God, and only love is what lives in your deepest heart. Feel that, and you will know God.

Some years ago, I became friends with a man who worked at a tea shop. Charles stood tall, with a tight, muscular physique. This gentle soul had dark skin and clear eyes that shone like two bright stars.

Charles was a practicing Hindu, with a smile that drew me close. He had read the *Bhagavad Gita* from front to back. He knew all its secrets. I knew nothing about his religion, but as we got to know each other, Charles recited from this book. He philosophized about love and about being one with all that breathes, and he talked about God.

Charles had a way of explaining God that made me hopeful that a life of unobscured unconditional love was possible. In his presence, I felt carefree, without the prickliness of the world poking at me.

Whenever I visited Charles at the tea shop, he took a break from behind the counter. Then we would make our way to a quiet corner to sit at one of the rickety wooden tables stained by mugs from previous tea drinkers. There he spoke about God, with conviction but without any religious dogma.

Charles's devotion to God encompassed many ideas, some of which I can't remember now. What stood out from our conversations, however, was that God is everywhere, always with us, and that so much of what can't be explained is also God.

I related to this loving unseen mystery that he said couldn't be explained. By the time I met Charles, I had been tapping into the bounty of the Universe through Tarot and channeling Guidance's wisdom, but God had never entered my sphere as it had his.

Being raised Jewish meant taking part in all the cultural holidays that brought friends and family together, yet a belief in God or even mentioning God was rare at these celebrations. I might have been around thirteen when I talked to my mom about God for the first time.

While she scrubbed the dinner dishes, I wiped down the wooden table with its high-gloss top after the five of us finished eating. We were alone by then. I asked her if she believed in God.

My mom shrugged, deflecting the question, her usual affect when she didn't want to engage with me. I bristled at her dismissive air, which felt like rejection—something I had become familiar with but never got used to.

I stopped my chore and leaned on the yellow Formica counter that separated us. Goading her for any reaction, I told her I didn't believe in any God because religions perpetuated hypocrisy, competition, and conflict around the world.

She stared out the kitchen window at the small rectangular patch of grass that was our backyard, saying nothing. I peered out onto that same evening's blackness from the window on my side.

We were both looking at the back of the dry-cleaning store that separated our two properties with a chain-link fence. During the day, white steam rose in billows and puffs into the sky. I often named the forms as if I were a farm kid looking up at clouds, instead of a city girl looking at an overgrown lot in the Bronx.

With the store closed that night, there were no steam formations to divert my attention. The uncomfortable silence grew between my mom and me along with the bitterness that lingered in our small house that she loathed, where I felt unappreciated and, at times, unloved.

My mom never answered my question. To this day, I have no idea if she believed in a God or not.

But Charles believed in God and talked in a way I never heard before that opened hearts to love. A love I recognized through Tarot and Guidance. I understood and felt this peaceful, unconditional acceptance that Charles described. I told him this.

Our difference, of course, was that Charles connected with God through religion. And Hindu or otherwise, religions are accepted conventions, unlike reading Tarot cards.

In the seventies, when I studied Tarot, the former status that this esoteric art once enjoyed had already been pushed underground, seen as an oddity. This was many years before Dior models strutted down the runway wearing dresses printed with images from the Mother Peace Tarot deck.

If I mentioned I read Tarot cards or received messages from Guidance, mouths literally dropped open. People looked at me without knowing what to say, then hurriedly changed the subject.

If I had been able to attribute my skills to a specific angel or someone like my wise dead grandmother, or if I called myself a psychic, then I would have appeared less weird and more acceptable.

After all, Sylvia Brown, a self-proclaimed medium and psychic, was a regular personality on the television talk-show circuits at that time. Folks couldn't get enough of her, including me. There was also Walter Mercado, an astrologer and psychic whose millions of fans on Spanish language television and radio worshipped him.

These two public figures although outspoken about their gifts, were also outspoken about their connection to God. I had no interest in depending on God to legitimize what I did, so I remained in the closet, too afraid of being judged.

But there was Charles who used the word "God" to talk about what both he and I understood as love. For the first time, I viewed God in a way relatable to what I knew. It shocked me even to consider the notion of God, to bring what had always been foreign to my senses close to my world.

I contemplated a belief in a God so that I would be accepted. After all, if God was love, maybe Guidance was a messenger from God? Maybe Guidance had been teaching me about God all along? Or maybe God is who I was channeling? Could God be my explanation for what I'd been doing?

Then one evening, as Charles and I shared dinner at my home, my tall friend challenged me to stop thinking about how to explain what Guidance and God were. He saw my analyzing as a distraction. He insisted I spend time deciding whether I could commit to love.

I had no doubt about my commitment to the Tarot and Guidance. Both taught me about love, by offering their love and reminding me to be more loving.

Maybe it was enough to accept that God for Charles and Tarot Guidance for me were transcendent mysteries. Did it matter if I couldn't explain the intangible I connected with? Did I really need God to legitimize what I had been doing all along? Did it matter what I called this indefinable source?

Years earlier, shortly after the first few messages from Guidance came through, I asked them to identify themselves. I needed a name. Their answer was unexpected.

You can call us Harry, or you can call us Sally. Call us whatever you like. Names are only a vibration.

Later I read or perhaps heard it from someone—that vocalizing the sound of "ah" as in God carries a vibration that, like rituals, has the potential to elevate our consciousness to an ethereal devotional place. Spelled either "Aum" or "Om" but pronounced the same, this holy syllable used in Buddhism also carries the "ah" sound. Pronounce the Bhagavad Gita, and the "ah" sound, is there as well.

Charles and I continued to have our disparate views about affiliating with a religion, but I came to accept his use of the term God. I understood that, for him, the word "God" was a synonym for love. This common spiritual understanding bonded us.

When Charles left town, we lost touch. Years later, I heard from a close friend of his that he died. I think about Charles now and again, and whenever I do, I'm able to summon his calming presence as if he were still here, with me.

Charles opened my eyes to how the religious pomp and circumstance I associated with God only served to divide and damage. Thinking about God through religion closed me off from accepting those who follow a religious belief with a pure loving heart.

Because of Charles, I softened my attitude. I figured the word "God," like "spirit," "source," or "higher power," explained the unexplainable.

Changing some of my views about God, however, didn't change my discomfort with using the actual word. Charles chose the word, as many people do, to describe this mystical unconditional source. But I can't shake how, in most Western cultures, God still carries too much religious lexicon, and therein lies the ultimate challenge.

God might be defined differently depending on one's religion, but the term is used in a way that leaves me doubtful that the word "God" could ever offer a universal nondenominational understanding about love that doesn't conjure an association to a specific religion. I believe in religious freedom, but to me, religions seem to separate and divide us instead of bringing us together through a common humanitarian understanding.

In the book, *The Power of Myth* (Doubleday, 1988), Joseph Campbell writes: "'God' is an ambiguous word in our language because it appears to refer to something that is known. But the transcendent is unknowable and unknown. God is transcendent, finally, of anything like the name 'God.'"

As Campbell expressed, once we name what is unknown, we have lost its true meaning. Guidance also points out that it's our relationship to the vibration that enables us to get closer to love.

Recently, while working with a client, Guidance insisted I use the word "God" during her reading. I cringed. The word sat between this woman and me as my discomfort grew, reminiscent of how, in the past, I played down being a Tarot reader for fear of being judged.

Would this woman reject me? I said nothing. She said nothing. I fidgeted with the cards on the table until I broke the silence. I told her I hoped the word had meaning for her. To my relief, she replied that it did.

The word "God" still has little if no meaning for me, but I no longer make the prejudicial assumption that when someone uses the word "God," they are a closed-minded religious fanatic. And when Guidance uses the word, I accept its relevance without worry or question.

Because of Charles, I came to think about God as I never had before and I'm grateful. I no longer view religion, God, and Guidance in opposition. There is a commonality for what Guidance wants that is no different from what any traditional religious "God" wants: for us to be immersed in love, inspired to love, so love spreads.

Reflections

Whether our wisdom and inspiration about love comes from a channeled spirit, a traditional religious practice, a belief in God, a deck of Tarot, or a set of oracle cards, it is up to each of us to love ourselves so we can remain close to this love that we know exists.

1. How do you relate to the word "God?" How do you relate to traditional religions?
2. Has your spiritual practice enabled you to connect to an unseen presence that is known to you?
3. As a seeker of spiritual insight, what do you believe is possible through the practice of loving yourself?

Traditional religions offer people community. A sense of belonging and validation. I, perhaps, like many of you, self-define what it is to be a spiritual seeker as we pursue a personal path that on occasion might feel isolating.

That's why we seek-out like-minded people, who identify with a "spiritual source" that doesn't fit into organized religious traditions. We need support. And yet, without common rituals, many of us can feel as if we're on a solo journey.

No matter what path we've chosen, the truth is that so many of the precepts that we follow, including what Guidance reveals in this book, are universal: acceptance, gratitude, letting go . . . to name a few.

We might understand these ideas in different ways, come to them in our own time, and incorporate them into our lives at varied stages, but all point to a more loving self and in this we have commonality.

I am heartened to think that the spiritual, non-religious community we are building is committed to ensuring that love remains the priority. This is our common ground. Ultimately what inspires us to love seems more important than defining who or what it is that offers us the opportunity.

14. Judgment

Judgment is protection.

Humans judge based on what they know, but what they know is limited by their experience.

You have learned to judge to protect yourself. But what do you protect yourself from?

It is wise to protect yourself from harm, it is true that your judgments can do this but protection from others is not always warranted.

Therefore, you should not accept your judgments without analyzing what you judge.

Judgment takes a thoughtful mind.

Do not judge others too quickly.

Do not judge others without all the facts.

Do not believe you have a right to judge others.

It is best to believe that without all the information, you can wait to judge.

It is best to believe that if you judge others, others can judge you.

It is best to believe that if you stop judging others, your heart will open.

You must know that once you do judge others, you have set in motion an aspect of life that could send you down a path of hate and hurt.

Mindful awakened understanding is what all judgments call for, and in this—all will be called to greater understanding.

Whenever I'm in Guidance's presence, whether with a client or connecting for my own purposes, the unconditional love that emanates comes through and there's not a judgmental thought that crosses my mind. This experience is true with Tarot cards too, which, like Guidance, never judge—ever.

You would think, after working with these tender, non-prejudicial sources for close to forty years, I would know better than to have judgmental thoughts during non-Tarot-Guidance hours when it's just me communing with myself. But you would be wrong.

My judgmental nature is quick to show its thorny side when I first meet someone. I decide within seconds whether I'm going to like them or not. Sometimes, my view is based on a general feeling I can't explain. At other times, I'm aware that I'm triggered by their looks, or what they said, or how they talked.

I feel horrible for doing this, especially when I watch other individuals embrace all kinds of people with diverse tastes, looks, and opinions.

The worst part is that although I notice my "judgy" thoughts as they happen, I don't stop them. I brush the observation aside, then resume my disapproving stance as if I were a victim of sudden amnesia. By the way, avoidance goes for how I sometimes respond to Guidance's wisdom. I spent many years choosing to ignore their prompting to deal with this specific issue.

Eventually, I realized I could no longer feign ignorance. I'm mortified every time I judge a total stranger, not to mention the psychic damage I do by criticizing myself for being judgmental.

Finally ready to change, I asked Guidance to help me. I got my wish unexpectedly one weekend at a mindful meditation workshop with about twenty other people. One of our first exercises turned out to be about judgment.

After lunch on the first day, the facilitator taped a blank piece of paper to our backs and handed us a sheet of sticky labels, each with pre-typed words. Staring back at me, I read "angry," "optimistic," "warm," "jealous," and plenty of other adjectives.

I hadn't been with these people long and didn't know anyone, but that didn't matter. We were instructed to mill about the room, then choose words—as many as we thought fit, to stick on the back of our fellow workshop-goer we thought deserving.

Everyone was squirming, including me. It's one thing to hold a judgment in confidence, quite another to let the person know you think they're "stubborn." One woman felt so uncomfortable that she said she wouldn't do the exercise. No one was excused.

As I sat waiting for the participants to receive their white sheets of paper and labels, I remembered how, after moving to rural Oregon from San Francisco, I met two conservative ranchers who I judged right away. I figured their politics would clash with my liberal views.

I had no interest in getting to know these men in their seventies, but my partner at the time felt different. She invited both to spend many afternoons sitting at our kitchen table or on our front porch.

They turned out to be kind gentlemen with huge hearts more accepting than mine. These crusty old Oregonians kept a fatherly watchful eye on us and never once judged us for being lesbians.

Recalling those years, I found myself questioning why that profound experience hadn't changed my judgmental heart for good. My musing was interrupted by the facilitator prompting us to turn our attention to the exercise at hand.

As I walked around the room, I placed one or two words on the backs of each person, convinced that my judgments were justified. But I wondered how I was making my decisions. Was I sizing up people based on their looks? Was it the inflection in their voice? Was it something they said that morning that I disagreed with? Was it his vibe? Her attitude? The fact that they weren't "my peeps"? What were my judgments really based on? I had never dug deep enough to get answers to those questions.

As we sat back in our seats, I looked at all the faces of the women and the one man I would be spending the next two days with. I felt ashamed and embarrassed. I didn't want to judge these people who were making themselves as vulnerable as myself, yet I found it easy to do so.

I focused on one woman sitting across from me. Earlier in the day, she offered information about her career along with being a wife and mother.

All morning she spoke with an eloquence I found appealing. No matter what she said, I found her thoughts insightful. I liked this woman. I wanted to get to know her. I even wondered if we could be friends.

As I stared in her direction, I felt shy. The confidence she exuded made me feel as if she were older than me, although I had no idea if this was true.

The awareness startled me, but I didn't allow it to stop me from investigating further. I felt diminutive compared to her, not in looks but in attitude, as if I were less capable than this woman. I believed she would think this about me as well and, therefore, wouldn't want to be friends.

How often had I done this in my life—been paranoid about being rejected?

I was bullied as a child. Name-calling was frequent. My limp and built-up shoe made me a target. My response to keep my head down and not look at others protected me from their stares and their judgments.

As my thoughts unwound, the final one landed with a thud. I hated being judged, but I had no qualms about judging others. *Eek!*

Guidance was right about judgment being a protection born of fear. I had to admit that I felt superior judging others before they could judge me, and this instinct had been my way of protecting myself. But this top-dog approach no longer made sense even though it's what I had been doing.

Tears flowed without expecting them, along with a sudden swell of sweetness for myself and those in the room that caught me off guard. My defenses were down. I kept others at a distance by judging them. I had adopted a coping mechanism that cost me and others a great deal of pain.

This eye-opening epiphany proved to be a game-changer, but I wasn't naive enough to think that *all* my judgments were based on my childhood traumas. Being judgmental is a human failing I'm guilty of regardless of the reasons.

Knowing this has made me more vigilant about my judgmental nature. So, unlike before, I am trying to change my behavior while it's happening . . . like the other day when I limped toward the counter at a coffee shop. I was aware of my usual embarrassment on the way I walked, noticing my concern about being judged by all the strangers in the room.

Did I want to feel inferior? Did I want to diminish others? As I waited in line to order coffee, I decided to test myself.

I spotted a woman wearing a flowered polyester dress sitting alone at a table. The old me wanted to judge her for wearing something I would never be caught in, but I only saw a stranger reading a book.

I scanned the room. I saw a mom with a toddler who I tried to criticize for allowing her kid to scream in a public place. Instead, I felt sympathy for how hard it must be to raise a child, something I know nothing about. And the guy with the beard— who, before the workshop, I would have mocked for looking unkempt—didn't bother me at all.

I had taken off my armor, surprised by how good it felt to be an equal in the crowd.

When I picked up my coffee, I hobbled toward the milk bar to add cream to my cup. In the past, I would have made my aura smaller by keeping my head bent with my eyes on the ground, unaware that my fear of being judged not only denied me pride but viewed everyone else as an enemy. Instead, I held my head high, met eyes straight-on, and smiled at every stranger I passed.

Reflections

Judgments require us to be more discerning than we sometimes are. After all, it's not like all judgments are bad. Many of our decisions are based on our sound judgments. Who would skydive without a parachute? But being thoughtful means becoming aware when our judgments get in the way, negatively affecting us or someone else.

1. How does it feel to be judged?
2. What might be different if you became aware of who and why you are judging?
3. What have your judgments cost you? What have they helped you with?

Usually, when I make a snap judgment about someone, what I am thinking isn't kind or generous. And when I'm critical of someone else, I can certainly come across as superior. That stance doesn't go down well with everybody. Nor should it.

I know people like this, too—those who judge others and are more than willing to express their judgments out loud but out of earshot of the person they are criticizing.

These behaviors might cause others to disassociate from us.

Why are we separating ourselves from each other? Our judgments keep people at a distance. Most of the time, we judge to cover our own insecurities. If this is true, that's a sad admission. But it's one begging us to heal.

15. Worry

Visualize worry like a cloud. Then blow it away.

Worry is not a lifestyle.

Worrying—to discern a problem, to figure out what you are worried about, to find solutions, to ask for help—this is what worry can offer.

Worry for worrying's sake keeps you stagnant, chained, and locked in a hell of your own making. Worrying for worrying's sake keeps you from taking action.

Keeps you in the grip of complaining.

Keeps you a victim of your own choosing.

Keeps you powerless to create solutions.

Like a hamster on a wheel, you will expend much energy getting nowhere.

When worry comes, ask for solutions. Ask the Universe to help you so that you can cycle away from worry. If solutions do not come right away, we ask that you trust and have faith that a solution will come, for solutions come without worry.

We ask that you notice when worry has encapsulated you, has taken over your moment, your day.

If you have no solutions for what your worry brings, we ask then that you accept how worry lives within. We ask you to notice, so you choose to suffer no more.

You can make worry like a cloud and blow it away.

We promise you can do this, and we promise you will feel better.

I grew up in a Jewish household without the stereotypical Jewish mother wringing her hands. My mom was a strong, no-nonsense, take-action woman. Typecasts be damned, it was my dad who was the worrier in our family, and he did it with a greatness I doubt few others could replicate.

When I moved from San Francisco to Eugene, Oregon, my dad who lived in Florida at the time sent a package by way of the postal service. He placed so many stamps of varying pictures and denominations that it looked like an avant-garde art piece. The parcel was flimsy. Its contents were contained in a department store-type of gift box, one that might hold a shirt wrapped in tissue paper rather than the heavy-duty corrugated cardboard you would expect from a package coming three thousand miles.

My dad's worry led him to fortify the box with brown wrapping paper and what looked like half a roll of silver duct tape, so nothing got lost, although one side came crushed. The haphazard appearance of the package didn't surprise me. It wasn't the first time in my life that I could not make sense of how his concerns led him to do such things.

When I got through all the tape, what had been sliding around was a small can of tick spray and an old plastic compass with a face so well-worn I could barely make out the symbols beneath the scratches. My dad knew I lived on a farm a mere ten miles outside the second-largest city in Oregon. Yet he imagined me living in the back-country where I would, undoubtedly, become lost and contract Lyme disease the minute I stepped out my front door.

My dad was oblivious to how worry affected him, but his worry affected me. His anxiety seemed a stressful way to live. He often woke me at five o'clock in the morning—eight o'clock his time—because he had finished his oatmeal with a side of worrisome thoughts and needed to know if my money was "safe" in my savings account.

Even when I answered with a positive response, he called me the next day with the very same question. He had heard my answer, but worrying came naturally, embedded in his personality. With a habit so unconscious, he had no choice but to repeat the same questions even when my tone of frustration got the better of me.

By the time Guidance sent me their message about blowing worry away like a cloud, I had witnessed my dad's high-end anxious uneasiness so many times (my entire life) that I didn't need much convincing. That didn't stop me from worrying, but it did motivate me to give their advice a try.

The first time I had a chance to practice blowing worry away occurred when my old '83 Volvo broke down in the parking lot of a natural food store a block from my home.

I had been running errands all over town that Sunday, so when the car gave up within walking distance to home, I felt grateful, although I also felt extremely bummed. I left a note on the windshield asking that the car not be towed.

First thing Monday morning, I called my mechanic Steve. He didn't answer. I relied on my car to get to work, so I left a message asking him if I could tow the car to his shop.

By nine-thirty, I still hadn't heard back. My dog Bow hadn't been walked because I had to stay inside to hear the phone ring. ("Sitting by the phone," was common before cell phones.)

Steve was an older gentleman with a one-man garage, which meant he made all the appointments, worked on all the cars, and ordered all the parts. The last time I saw him, he talked about slowing down and retiring.

What if Monday was his day off? What if he did retire? What if I couldn't get my car back in time to go to work? I had not budgeted a loaner. What if something major like a timing belt or a new alternator was the problem? Those fixes were expensive.

My worried thoughts piled on. The clock in the kitchen read ten-thirty. I had to be at work by one. I didn't know what to do. I paced around my house like a trapped animal.

Worry wasn't even a thing anymore. I was in full panic mode, too stressed to think clearly.

What had Guidance said about how nothing gets solved by worrying? I sat down at my kitchen table. I needed to feel settled instead of at odds. I calmed down so I could think.

Within moments, I remembered clipping an advertisement for a new auto shop in town that specifically mentioned Volvos. I found the ad tacked to my bulletin board and called the number. By eleven-thirty, there was a tow-truck whisking my car, my dog, and me to their garage.

The fix proved to be easy and inexpensive. I drove away with enough time to take Bow for a long walk, run an errand I had been putting off, and get to work.

I learned something useful that day. As Guidance describes, finding solutions gets easier when my head isn't filled with the distracting mumble-jumble of worry.

Since then, I've become more in tune with how worry affects me. I have also noticed how even those who are well-meaning can exacerbate my worry by adding their reasons for why I "should" be worried. This has made me think twice about who I share my worry with.

Knowing this, however, hasn't made me immune from adding to someone else's worry. Like the time my neighbor wanted to rebuild his garage. I took Jim's worry and ran with it.

When Jim told me he was caught in the bureaucracy of our city's permit office, I went on about the unjust system and how he would spend thousands of dollars more than he initially planned. I felt it my duty to point this out as if he hadn't already known.

I couldn't mistake the anxious look on Jim's face. I have no doubt I added to his worry, which doubled his worry distress. Lesson learned. We all have enough stress in our lives. I know I do.

I took prednisone for over a year brought on by the pain of Polymyalgia Rheumatica, a medical condition specifically brought on by high stress. My dad, on the other hand, who elevated worry to an art form, remained a healthy specimen his entire life until he died from a fall at ninety-two.

His worry never caused ulcers, migraines, high blood pressure, or Polymyalgia Rheumatica. Think of my father like an albino kangaroo—so rare you'll never see another one like it again in your lifetime.

Obviously, I did not inherit my dad's "worry doesn't stress me out" genes. My worry keeps me up at night when I would rather be sleeping instead of dealing with acid reflux. However, Guidance has made me aware that worrying for worrying's sake truly is a waste of my time.

That's the reason I pick up a book, or play a game on my tablet, or listen to music when I can't quiet that inner voice at four in the morning. I have found that diverting my thoughts is a welcome solution when blowing worry away like a cloud isn't as easy as it sounds.

Reflections

Worrying doesn't make us more in control of our situation. It can actually make us less in control, especially when our thoughts are churning without finding solutions. Worry can contribute to feelings of powerlessness.

1. Are there certain topics you worry about repeatedly?
2. How does worrying impact you or the quality of your life?
3. What are some of your *go-tos* that lessen or relieve your worry? Meditation? Obtaining problem-solving advice from friends or experts? Imagining worry to be as light as a cloud so you can blow it away?

When I'm in a spin cycle of worry, I've tried willpower to stop my thoughts, but that doesn't work. What can work is tuning into my body's reaction to worry, observing it as if I were someone else.

With this focus, worry feels like its own entity, vibrating and tumbling around like a creature living within me, but not a part of me, yet I am the one sitting in discomfort. I am the one vibrating. I am the one who isn't calm.

I breathe in and out, witnessing, certain I don't like feeling this way. Will I continue to suffer?

This question is enough to lessen worry's dense hold until, eventually, it does evaporate. When I remember to do this exercise, Guidance's declaration always resonates louder. Worrying for worry's sake is a waste of my time.

16. Comparison

*Comparing yourself to another is the best way to lose sight
of who you are and what you uniquely offer.*

Comparison blinds you to your true gifts.

You can never know who you truly are or what you truly want when you compare.

Comparison means someone is better and someone is worse.

This is not a fair judge.

This is not an objective understanding.

When you compare, you are either the winner or the loser. If you pick the winning side, you are blinded by feeling better about yourself due to another. If you have chosen to be the loser, you are shaming yourself into what is less than who you are. Either way, love for self cannot get through.

One cannot compare and feel good about self, for comparisons, pick at people, pulling them apart from one another.

When you compare, you choose to suffer, for in that state, you are not true to yourself. And when you are not true to self, you will never see your greatest gifts, for no comparison can show you that.

Comparing only shows what you are not.

If you are wise and aware of the comparisons you make, you can learn much because this realization will bring you back to yourself.

You do not need to compare yourself as a motivation to do better. You can decide to change yourself and your circumstances based on what you agree needs to change. Your time is better spent on these pursuits than comparing yourself to another.

True acceptance of self will come by releasing comparisons, so we ask that you love yourself more and let the pettiness of your comparing obsession go.

I was four or five years old when I stood on a crowded street corner in the Bronx holding my sister's hand. While we waited for the light to turn green, an older kid yelled above the crowd, "Hey, why are you wearing that big shoe, small fry?" My left saddle shoe had a built-up sole as weighty and thick as a brick. I knew that kid was talking about me, and I remember lowering my head, embarrassed.

This is my first memory of being singled out as different. It wouldn't be the last time. Unfortunately, over the years, I internalized how being different meant there was something wrong with me.

I went from being a self-conscious child to a self-conscious adult. In a society that puts a high value on how women are supposed to look, I endlessly compared myself to others—those who could put the finishing touches on a sexy dress with a pair of heels instead of the sensible lace-up shoes with the clunky lift I needed to wear.

In my late thirties, I questioned the many hours I logged comparing myself to others. Not measuring up was as normal a feeling and as daily a routine as brushing my teeth or locking my front door.

Guidance's wisdom felt accurate. Comparison served no purpose and had become as wearisome as searching for a parking spot in Midtown Manhattan.

This self-effacing custom was on my mind the morning I arrived at Breitenbush Hot Springs Retreat. This beautiful oasis, where roaming naked is the norm, is located on private wooded land along Oregon's McKenzie River. I preferred being naked in hot tubs, but on the drive up, I was already stressing about the stares that awaited when the scars on my leg and back curved from scoliosis were no longer hidden by clothes.

After soaking in one of the outside hot tubs, which I grate-fully had to myself, I decided to check out the sauna. The wooden structure was shaped like an igloo and about as small.

People were packed in, but to my relief, I found an empty spot on one of the three long benches lining the walls. I sat down carefully to avoid touching the sweaty thighs of my neighbors on both sides.

In the tight, enclosed space, it proved impossible to avoid looking at other people. I scanned the benches of naked men and women. Whether they were fat, thin, hairy, or hairless, their bodies appeared normal, unlike mine.

As the steam rose, I looked down at my small scarred left leg, atrophied foot and toes, and ribs that protruded, rotating so far to the right that, years earlier, a kid likened me to Quasimodo. I couldn't stop looking, thinking, comparing. It didn't take long before my self-conscious anxiety overshadowed what was supposed to be a pleasant, relaxing experience. I stood to leave.

Once outside on the deck, I gratefully found my towel hang-ing on the hook where I left it. I wrapped the cotton around me. I was alone, but the habit of hiding my body came instinctually.

I watched the sun set behind the evergreen trees that bor-dered the property. As the glow disappeared, the bright blue sky turned to shades of gray.

The land fell quiet. Those in the sauna became quiet too as if they were like the songbirds I'd heard during the day, who now, had gone silent as well, their instinct to stop chirping when evening comes.

The temperature dropped, but I remained hot from the sauna. With no one around, I discarded my towel. I sat down naked, amazed at my own courage.

Content and lost in my own world, I rested my misshapen leg on the bench out in front of me. I examined every scar. My fingers carefully smoothed over every indentation. I looked closer with more focused intention at what lay before me than I had ever done before.

As I stared at my leg with its irregularities, I heard Guidance's loving voice.

I'm not sure what brought on my pensive mood that evening. Maybe the sudden stillness of the land. Maybe finding myself alone; a welcomed gift after being around people all day. Maybe it was the sanctity of the gray cast that protected me as night approached. But after so many years of comparing myself to others, I let down my guard along with the tension of self-loathing I carried. I was open to what Guidance had to say.

You're perfect.

I looked again at my small, marred leg, then lifted my good leg up on the bench too. They were side by side. Both legs were mine. Both legs had always been mine. Both legs were part of me.

Why did I measure myself against others? Why have I made my body, the one I inhabit, my enemy?

I looked at my left leg again, with an ownership and acceptance I had never known. Instead of turning away to reject the flaws, I continued to stare, filled with a kindness that was long overdue.

I used to see my difference as a detraction rather than appreciating how it makes me who I am. I see now how this outlook kept me distant from loving myself and certainly prolonged a cycle of self-hate.

What eluded me for far too long—what I refused to embrace until that evening at Breitenbush—was pride. Every one of us is unique and being unique is a birthright we all share whether disabled or not.

Reflections

Making comparisons tends to pit us against one another. When we consider ourselves inferior to someone else, this might motivate us to improve. Or, if we believe we're better than somebody, perhaps we would become humble. The reality, however, is quite different. When we compare, we only create winners and losers.

Some self-reflection can help you avoid making these comparisons. Ask yourself:

1. What do you accomplish when you compare yourself to someone else? Do you gain anything? What do you lose?
2. How does comparing yourself to other people make you feel?

When we remain unaware of the comparisons we make or ignore how they affect us, we aren't doing ourselves any favors. Taking time to reflect on this issue might lead to a more loving self as we find personal acceptance that is, perhaps, long overdue.

17. Death

Death is only as it was always meant to be.
Part of life. Part of your life path.

You all have death in common, so why the concern? There is nothing on the other side that can hurt you.

Only once in a lifetime will you have this opportunity, and only once in a lifetime, you will live this death.

The mystery is the fulfillment. The understanding that death as a part of life is your birthright, as the sand, sea, and shore are yours to wonder at. Wonder about death, but do not allow it to interfere with life.

There are no questions that can be answered about death.

The mystery is half the fun.

The other half is to live.

One's sadness to lose life is real. The sadness of feeling how life goes by is real. Sadness is not your enemy but a friend that reminds you to live in compassion for self and others. Sadness only reminds you to be human. To make a life of love even more filled with love.

Death cannot stop love. Time cannot erase love. Living is what expresses love. Through life, one can have love. Being love is the true gift.

Every day you die a little more and every day you get closer to death. One's life, when done, no matter the time or place, is what all have in common.

An end to life is only the beginning, for cycles of life and love are infinite. No matter the ripple you make, the effect is broad. Make your ripple wisely. The stone you cast is infinite.

Death will certainly show its many faces to you in this lifetime and is a shared experience, as no one will leave this world whole. But, in that, you

*all have one another, and so this shared experience should be your greatest
teacher to love one another.*

*Share not in the misery of your deaths but in the acknowledgment of
your lives. Live together well. Share together in song. Love together in heart,
so when you die, your ripple of love remains.*

I've always been afraid of death. The unimaginable idea that
my life will no longer exist scares me to my core. I literally
shake when I picture myself lowered into a grave or burned at
fourteen hundred degrees Fahrenheit.

I was around eight when I first asked my mom about death.
I don't remember what prompted my curiosity, but we were
sitting next to each other on the couch in our living room when
I wanted to know if she was going to die.

"We all die," she said.

I remember wobbling her dangling triceps back and forth
with my fingers, realizing for the first time that she was older, in
a category not unlike my grandma.

"Even me?" I questioned.

"Yes, even you," she said.

The thought then, like now, remains incomprehensible. I
have not yet resolved my feelings about what Guidance insists
is the natural order.

When friends tell me they're certain they're coming back
after they die, I'm supportive of their belief even though I'm
not one hundred percent convinced that reincarnation is a real
thing. It's not that I completely rule out the possibility; it's
just that I find the whole notion impossible to wrap my head
around fully.

I listen as friends describe their past lives while secretly roll-
ing my eyes. Then I have the nerve to remember that I too have
had visions of a past life or two. It's a conundrum, but I accept

this paradox of my uncertain view about what happens after death because death is the ultimate uncertainty.

I once asked Guidance if we know when we are going to die or how. They answered *yes*, that we all know but are afraid to know. They told me that it's our fear of death that keeps us ignorant of the specifics of how and when we die.

I play with wanting to know. I asked Guidance about my own death but received no answer. After contemplating the idea for a while—car accident, sudden heart attack, cancer—my fears about the what, the when, the how, and that I'll be gone make my brain shut down. Once again, I avoid thinking about my ultimate end.

Nevertheless, some people intuitively know when they're going to die even if they can't put their finger on the specifics. Years ago, a friend's dad told her he hoped that when it was his time, he would be doing what he loved best: skiing. Sometime later, they found his body slumped against a snowy tree in the middle of a downhill run.

I also wonder if it might be possible to will ourselves to die if it's what we consciously want. Aunt Lil and Uncle Morris were one of the most in-love couples I knew growing up. I was a teenager when Aunt Lil had a stroke that put her in a coma. My uncle visited her at the nursing facility every day for five years until she died. He died less than a month after her.

I believe the one truth about death is that—no matter whether we feel peaceful at the end of our lives or are afraid right up to our last breath—our death will be personal; we'll have only ourselves. Even with our loved ones around us, dying is a solo activity. And like my friend's father, we face death, whatever it is, however it comes, alone.

Oregon has a Death with Dignity Act. My husband's father, an immigrant from Poland, chose this alternative. Tony knew he would suffer from the fast-approaching pain of prostate cancer and the increased dosages of morphine that would certainly hold his mind and body hostage as his last days drew near.

His decision, while he was still in fair health and of sound mind, was to choose his own day and time. Dressed in his best suit and tie, he lay on the couch. While his sons, daughter, and wife watched, he took enough pills to fall asleep forever.

When I mull over the long list of possibilities for my own demise—heavy tree limb, rockslide, drowning—the idea of suicide and being in control of my fate, rather than carrying around the burden of wondering, helps me to understand why some, like my father-in-law, would want to control their own death.

Carolyn Heilbrun, a retired Columbia University literary scholar, took death into her own hands at seventy-seven. In an article I read while researching suicide on the web, Ms. Heilbrun's son said, "She felt her life was a journey that had concluded." He confirmed that his mother was not sick when she took her own life.

Writers Jerzy Kosiński, Ernest Hemingway, and Sylvia Plath along with Robin Williams, Kate Spade, and Anthony Bourdain all chose to end their life on their terms. A good friend did, too. Brian was in his early fifties when he decided it was time to close the door on his life.

We can weigh in on whether each person was actually in control or just caught in a single moment of wavering mental health, but how do we really know? Faced with death, whether through choice or having no choice at all, can any of us say with certainty that we are in our right minds? What does it take in human terms to greet this final moment, to know you will live no longer?

My husband, unlike me, has no fear of death. He has zero belief in an afterlife and is sure that when we die, we are done, finished, and asleep without consciousness or memory. No before or after. Nothingness. In short—dead.

I envy my husband's straightforward, no-nonsense, no-contemplation calm stance that nothing awaits us after death. I, on the other hand, am consumed by thoughts about my death, due to fear. How will I die? What happens when I die? Where will I be? Fear.

I know I'm not the only person who is afraid to die. The world's religions, including Buddhism, offer ways to help their followers grapple with death.

Religions try to prepare us. Do good in this lifetime so you are guaranteed placement in the next realm. Stay conscious of your losses so each little death here prepares you for the big one. Or you won't be alone after death because loved ones, angels, or your savior are waiting for you.

As Guidance points out, religion is only capable of making death appear less scary because no religion can offer quantifiable information about the death experience. Therefore, what am I to believe about death?

I believe that death is one of only two experiences that qualify as the most life-altering for a person; having a child is the other. But unlike bringing a newborn home, we'll receive no pamphlets with the all-important information plus instructions needed so we know what to expect when we're dead.

I once did a Tarot Guidance reading for a young woman in her late twenties who had an incurable illness. She knew her time was limited—a thought she lived with every day. During her session, she asked me about her death. What came through for her was no different from what Guidance tells all of us.

Death is the experience you all share.

No matter our age, no one is getting out of this life alive. The reminder that death has been in existence for as long as humans have walked this earth comforted this young woman in the moment, as it does me at times.

My hope is that, at the end of my life, I might find it easier to embrace death by understanding that my individual life isn't that precious. Certainly not precious enough to live forever, even if that were possible.

I'm a blip in this world, a speck in a cosmos greater than me. When I die, I'll be making room for someone else on this planet. I will be doing what all have done before me. No better, no worse, just the same. Death comes for all of us, the ultimate leveling of the playing field.

Yet even knowing my life ends the same as it does for everyone, I can't seem to escape the fact that anytime I contemplate my death, it's a downer. During those times, Guidance tries to lift my spirits by reminding me that today matters. That what I do while I'm alive is what matters. Being compassionate matters. Helping others matters. Being kind matters.

I only wish I could remember these ideals as I go through my day, the ones Guidance suggests we keep alive by thinking about death, because then I might live every moment with more wonder, more gratitude, and maybe I would smile at people more often.

The truth is that during my waking hours, I rarely think about death and its lessons—to live as if today were my last. I have far too much fear to dwell there.

Besides, my grandparents and parents lived well into their nineties. I figure with their genes on my side, I have plenty of years left to find a peaceful resolution with the Grim Reaper should I live that long.

Reflections

Perhaps your spiritual belief about death provides you with comfort. Or maybe, like me, you are afraid to die. Or maybe, like my husband, you have zero fear. Regardless of our beliefs, death is woven into the fabric of our lives. Therefore, contemplating our personal philosophy and belief on the subject might be valuable.

1. How do thoughts about death impact your life?
2. What do you believe happens after death?
3. Guidance teaches that the life we are living now is the one to make the most of. Is there anything that might change or something you might do differently if you thought about your life in this way?

Sometimes I wonder what it would be like if I talked to friends about death as much as I talk about my business, love-life, or finances. But I never can bring up the topic. How do I jump from listening to a girlfriend's experience at a new job to asking about her views on death? What's a natural segue to that conversation?

And yet talking about death might be a good thing. I know people who left this earth without putting their finances in order due to their own misgivings about death.

Many cultures do accept death's inevitability and have ritualized the experience with celebration. Mexico's Day of the Dead comes to mind.

Of course, there is no guarantee that, if I found ways to celebrate death, this would erase my fears or motivate me to write my will. But experience has shown that talking openly about taboo topics tends to neutralize their impact or if nothing else, takes away some of the sting.

18. Grief

A place that begins to heal what it is you have lost.

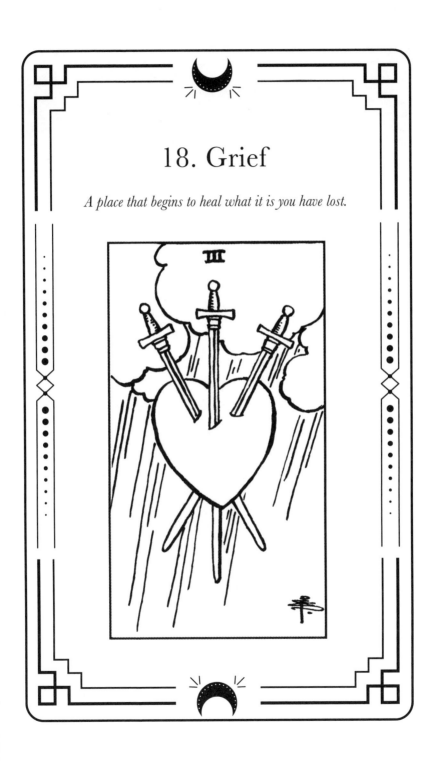

Grief is about what you miss. What you've lost. Sometimes it's about a person; sometimes it just is. In its purest form, it is not about the one who has passed over or the thing that is lost. It is about what one feels about the loss.

Missing is your grief.

That you have loved, a person, a pet, even a thing is why your grief comes. Yet as time moves forward, loss is also every moment in your life.

Why is it, then, that grief is universal, yet you do not give it its due, or its understanding.

For as long as you feel grief, you must accept its expression. Releasing grief is a healthy expression of love.

Grief is the tie that binds your memory to what or who you miss.

Do not be afraid to grieve, for when you express grief, it will lessen in time. It is only when you refuse to feel grief that it stays waiting to surprise you.

Respect your grief time, and do not allow others to decide how much grief is enough. Grief is a personal journey, and all would do well to remember this.

Allow grief to wash over you when you feel the need and, in so doing, you will remember just how much love you feel in your own heart.

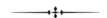

Some years back, I went through a period of spontaneous crying that I couldn't explain. I cried at work, in my car, or while pushing a grocery cart. These crying jags came without warning.

My inability to control when and where I cried reminded me of another time when I wept in public. I was about fourteen, sitting alone, on top of a grassy hill in "Pidgeon Park," a favorite local hangout in my neighborhood. A group of teens walked by and laughed at me. I was "too sensitive," they shouted. Their ridicule put an immediate kibosh on my bawling around people.

But now I had no choice. I couldn't stop my tears, although I wanted to.

When a friend or a coworker asked why I was upset, I had no response. I didn't know the cause, but at the same time, I gave into the grief that followed me wherever I went.

There is an understanding in Jewish tradition that the grieving process takes time. Mourners are supported for a full year when someone dies. This one-year cycle offers the opportunity to experience the first holidays, birthdays, and other celebrations without a loved one present. This also means we have permission to do whatever we need.

My Aunt Irene knew this. When I visited her about nine months after my Uncle Irv died, I asked her to play the piano for me, something I looked forward to when I saw her. Without hesitating and without an apology, she refused me in a clear matter-of-fact tone, "I'm still mourning," she said.

I was in my early twenties when we buried my grandpa. During the first year of his death, like my Aunt Irene, I had the same response to friends who asked for a favor or some "hang time." Without guilt or apology, I said "no."

My current sadness felt similar. When I couldn't put on a happy face, I turned down many requests without offering an excuse or worrying about the repercussions.

Yet even with my resolve to cry wherever and whenever, I wanted to make sense of my grief. I needed to understand what was happening to me.

I tested all the possibilities. I thought about my dead grandparents. Was I grieving for them? I thought about dead friends, pets, and the loss of my mobility as a child, along with the many relationship breakups that left me bereft. None of these memories evoked the deep sadness I felt. Then Guidance clued me in.

Humans need to release what is pent up inside. Releasing grief, no matter the cause, expels toxins and is a healthy expression—an important expression.

Their information brought awareness. It did feel as if I was partaking in a good cleanse by releasing pent-up energy sitting within me. But I also had an inkling, due to the enormity of my experience, that I might also be shedding the world's heartache, perhaps a distress held for decades, possibly centuries. One I'd absorbed, taken in, resting inside of me for far too long. I allowed for this explanation. It made sense. It felt right.

As I looked past my own grief, I became sensitive to how uncomfortable many of us are while witnessing each other's tears. Who wants to be reminded of so much pain? Maybe the waterworks I showed on that hill long ago tapped into the pain of those who wanted me to stop. The pain of grief is painful to watch.

I wept uncontrollably for one whole week, wondering when my misery would end. And then it did as abruptly as it began.

When it was over, I felt raw and tired, but relieved of a burden I had no idea I carried. I walked with a lighter step, more in my body, more centered with a sense of contentment I hadn't experienced in a long while.

Perhaps we all carry a level of grief lying below the surface that every so often begs our attention. I needed those tears to flow. Maybe we all do at times.

Reflections

Some people don't allow themselves to express grief. One reason they give is that if they start crying, they will never be able to stop crying. I haven't googled this, but I doubt anyone has ever drowned in their own tears.

I would agree that grief isn't an easy-breezy feeling. There's emotional distress, not to mention the crying headaches, the endless tissues, and our sense of exhaustion. But grief is one of our many emotions, so maybe all we really need to do is figure out how to take better care of ourselves and each other when we do grieve.

1. What messages have you received about the appropriateness or inappropriateness of crying?
2. How do you view the experience of grief?
3. What is gained or hindered by putting time limits on the grieving process, either for you or someone else?

If it's true that toxins are released by a grief cleanse, then finding ways to expel grief periodically might be as healthy as an annual liver flush. Instead of drinking an herbal mix, however, maybe a sad song, heart-wrenching poem, or something sappy on YouTube could kick-start a weepy mood. I haven't needed to try this yet, but next time I feel all choked up, these ideas will be worth considering.

19. Abundance

Abundance is your heart calling.

Abundance is not about a thing. It is not about wanting. It is not about having.

It is about you and what you value.

But what does one value? One can only value what is in one's heart.

What is in one's heart is love.

Abundance is your heart made bigger.

A big heart holds all of what your life has to offer.

A big heart can hold all of the love you have to offer.

When you focus on abundance, you can feel the power of its teachings. Abundance is a life that has meaning. Purpose will find you, but meaning is yours to create.

Each life is meaningful, and in this, you are already abundant. You are already huge with love.

Abundance is the thought that will have you reaching for more of who you are and what you can be while you allow for the abundant creature you are today.

Your abundant loving heart will guide you. Let it.

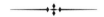

Last spring, I redecorated my office. I ordered a decal with the word "abundance" in a pleasant script. I figured if I stuck the word on my wall, it would inspire my money-making mojo.

After offering Tarot Guidance for forty years and retiring from my last day job, I decided to create a bona-fide business. The transition wasn't easy. Focusing on readings as a way to earn a living had always caused me concern.

It wasn't that I thought paying for my time was unwarranted. I charged, but from the very beginning, I felt uncomfortable when I viewed Tarot Guidance through money-making eyes.

I always relied on day jobs to support myself, yet throughout the years, I remained heavily influenced by well-meaning friends who encouraged me to make more money with my Tarot Guidance skill.

As I placed the decal on my wall, I hoped the word "Abundance" could overshadow my misgivings. I wanted to embrace this new commercial enterprise. But once again, my discomfort about making money a priority butted up against my natural inclination to ignore the focus on finances.

All this was going on in my head when I heard Guidance's voice.

Abundance is about creating a life where you are centered on how big your life already is.

I allowed for this new idea about abundance to penetrate— how it encapsulated the entirety of my life. As this became clearer, I saw the word "wealth" separate from the word "Abundance." The two words hung independently from one another, distinct, like two separate paintings drawn by two very different artists.

"Abundance," not "wealth," held my gaze as the great weight of my internal conflict shifted. Sure, financially, things could always be better, but on the whole, I had no complaints.

I recognized how my life *was* already "abundant," overflowing with profuse goodness. I wrapped this truth into the core of my being.

I had wonderful friends, a great husband, love from family, and the skill of reading Tarot Guidance, which I embraced as an act of service, never having refused anyone a reading if they couldn't afford to pay.

I also included the personal changes I made over the years. After a life filled with wicked self-doubt and low self-esteem, I grew to believe in my own value. A very abundant gift, I might add.

It struck me that my conflict about money and Tarot Guidance had everything to do with value. I had never realized this, but I had given in to societal pressures about my self-worth being tied to making money. If I dismissed money's value with Tarot Guidance, this somehow implied how little I valued myself. *Geesh!*

I went to my bulletin board to rip up all the documents associated with my business plan. I gave credence to what I instinctively knew—that making enough money to support myself through readings had never been a priority and never would be.

The inner turmoil I held for so long was over. I took the "abundance" sign off my wall and threw it in the trash. Abundance and its expansive nature were at work in my life every day. I didn't need a decal to remind me.

Reflections

My definition of the word "abundance" used to be solely linked to material wealth. Although this is one aspect, equating abundance solely with money was short-sided. Guidance counsels that abundance is a holistic way to view life. When we view our life as abundant, this allows us to see how being alive is an abundant gift and how the Universe is an abundant place.

1. Other than material items, what areas of your life feel abundant?
2. What might be different if you recognized abundance throughout your day, every day?

Guidance states that "abundance" defines an outlook that delivers more impact to our lives than dollars and cents ever could. Therefore, recognizing abundance more broadly and more often, is a good way to open our eyes to the infinite potential that exists for all of us.

20. Choice

When faced with a choice, please remind self that you can choose again.

We cannot say what a choice can hold for you other than knowing all choices will teach you. Use your choices and see them with awareness.

Choice isn't your enemy. Choice is your gift. Choice is not your hell to pay but your greatest rise to consciousness.

Freedom lies in consciousness.

Consciousness equals freedom.

Conscious choices offer you freedom.

Freedom is about being fully aware of the decisions made by you rather than decisions being made for you through your fear or ignorance.

Ignorance and fear cannot set you free. Ignorance and fear keep freedom away. Ignorance and fear keep you away from freedom of movement.

Choices made with full awareness, those made from your full self of knowing, will never fail you.

When one chooses with awareness, freedom is present and, therefore, there are no wrong choices.

Awareness guides your choices. Love directs your actions. There are choices in life that will change your course forever. Judging them is futile.

Some years back, I worked as a salesperson at a music store where I could put my musical knowledge to good use. I helped customers choose the best metronome, buy a percussion instrument for their toddler, or suggest a music book that offered more interest, depending on the person's experience.

I enjoyed going to a job where I schmoozed with professional musicians, symphony, and jazz players, along with music teachers and hobby players eager to purchase their first instrument. I looked forward to walking through the door for my eight-hour shift, five days a week, until my second year. That's when my boss's micromanagement style started to wear thin.

This manager's overbearing, controlling attitude might have been understandable if the employees were incompetent, but that wasn't the case. All the sales staff and tech guys who repaired instruments knew their jobs, were friendly to customers, and got their work done. Yet for some reason, this manager found it necessary to criticize. Unfortunately, too often, this happened at the front counter where everyone could hear. Morale at the store was low.

I planned to give notice when I started to date my current husband. Falling in love with Johnny proved to be such a distraction that searching for a new job lost its appeal. It didn't take long, however, before I was dragging my ass to work again.

The second time I decided to quit, I found out I had breast cancer. The store provided good health insurance, so I worked there for another two years, longer than I would have preferred.

During that period, I complained frequently to Johnny. I railed against my situation. I hated being at the store.

I felt trapped until it dawned on me that I made the decision to stay. I chose to sacrifice my happiness for the medical attention I needed. With that understanding, I experienced a shift and what Guidance teaches: that choices made in consciousness equals freedom.

I stopped blaming the store manager for my miserable predicament. I went from feeling like a victim to feeling empowered by my sound decision.

My newfound attitude still didn't make going to work any more fun, but beating cancer was my priority. Remembering, made the long challenging days at the store possible and got me up and out the door in the morning without resentment.

Periodically, I tested my choice to continue at a job where I felt dissatisfied. To do this, I fantasized about quitting. But each time I thought I might follow through my answer remained an unshakable "not today." I remained in the driver's seat of my decision, knowing, that at some point, I would have a different response.

That day came when my health crisis was over. I gave my two weeks' notice without a moment of hesitation and without one regret for those years I remained.

Reflections

Life is a series of choices. Even when we can't decide, we are making a choice. We sometimes judge our choices, perceiving them as "good" or "bad." And often we believe we have "no choice," which upon examination, isn't always the truth.

The reality is that making choices with our full awareness means we are the ones directing our life. This enables us to endure any sacrifice we might be making. This also means we take responsibility. And taking responsibility for our choices makes it harder to fall victim to our circumstances.

1. How do you reflect on a choice and how do you know when you are choosing?
2. When you are unable to make a choice, what helps you to move forward?

Clients often come to me when faced with a decision they are uncertain about. I understand this. We can find it challenging to make a choice, especially when we don't want to make the wrong one or we're caught up in the *shoulds* or the *what ifs*.

It's been my experience that once all the confusing noise is out of our way, most people in fact know what they want. At that point, whatever fear held us back dissipates so we become braver and can fully take in Guidance's reminder, that no matter what we choose, we can choose again.

21. Fear

*Fear can overwhelm, but taken in
small bites, it is manageable.*

Positive thoughts create positive action. But positive thoughts can be blocked by what one fears.

What you fear is often hard to recognize and so it overwhelms you. But fear is something you can understand. And once fear is named, it becomes smaller.

All humans experience fear.

The idea of working with fear is to understand what you fear.

Once you are awake to the cause of your fear, you can make the choice to consciously remove the block that prevents you from getting a better job, experiencing the abundance you've wished for, or accepting the loving relationship you've been dreaming about, or doing what makes you feel better instead of living with fear.

If you are blocked from the successes you want, if you are asking but still not receiving—fear might be the reason.

You can befriend fear. You can learn to walk with fear, holding its hand so it does not override a decision that is better for you. A decision made with the awareness that fear exists will allow you to move mountains.

Fear of looking the fool, fear of asking for love, fear that you're irresponsible with money. Once known, once named, fear becomes smaller; no longer large, like a bear you have to wrestle to the ground. Fear then becomes a porcupine that you can learn how to work around.

"Feel the fear and do it anyway" are strong words in your world. But you will remain stuck since these words are meaningless if you do not recognize and name the fear that stops you.

Breathe into fear to calm its head, for at that moment, it cannot harm you. Learn to look deep at what scares you.

When you are clear about what you fear, we ask that you hold the hand of self as you would a scared child. Fear itself may still exist. But as you walk in awareness holding fear's hand, you will find comfort, as you would comfort a child, and you will be moved toward greater things.

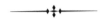

One of my shortcomings is that I'm slow to finish projects I've started. The book I've borrowed won't get read until my friend wants it back. Craft projects sit for years. Tasks on my to-do list will undoubtedly show up on my next list and the one after that.

Doing most everything at a snail's pace bugs me, especially when I am excited about something I am working on—like this book, for example. As passionate as I was about this project, even with my desire to get it done, I operated in my usual procrastination mode instead of in productive mode.

Pages don't write themselves. So, after avoiding my computer on yet another day, I wondered if something else might be going on that contributed to my stalling. Guidance responded.

What are you afraid of?

Was fear getting in my way? My answer came. What if I do all this work on the book and the finished copy has no life outside of my computer?

Ah, there it was again. Fear of being disappointed. My inability to deal with any disappointment was a big button-pusher for me, which proved to be problematic since it had me avoiding all sorts of goals.

Like the time I wanted to date but was so afraid of being disappointed by the masses who, I imagined would surely reject me, it took another two years to find the courage. Now I avoided writing. I wanted the book published but felt certain it would never be read by anyone but me. The fear of disappointment settled within me.

I asked new questions. Would I allow disappointment to win? Would I continue to let fear of being disappointed sabotage my progress? Besides, if I never finished the book, how would I know if I would be disappointed by its lack of readership?

I liked these thoughts. I was being rational. But I knew from experience that willpower alone couldn't motivate me to write. If I didn't give my fear of being disappointed its due, I would continue to make coffee dates with friends instead of climbing the stairs to my office.

What experience had caused disappointment to be so scary that avoidance became my coping mechanism?

From the time I began to walk, I wore a left shoe with a bulky lift to make up for the difference in the length of my legs. At nine years old the doctor promised I would be able to wear high heels in my teens if I had surgery to correct the discrepancy. My parents were all for it. I don't remember agreeing to the surgery or giving my consent, but I walked away from that visit with a lighter step, filled with hope that I'd look "normal" like everyone else.

I woke up from that surgery permanently disabled, with physical problems far worse than wearing a two-and-a-half-inch lift on my shoe. I still remember the morning the surgeon stood at the foot of my hospital bed, discharging me from his care because there was nothing more he could do. I hid my devastation. I didn't cry, but his words sunk me.

The doctor never apologized for his inability to deliver on the assurance that I would be "fixed." My parents avoided the subject altogether; perhaps they too couldn't handle the disappointment. I may never know what prompted their avoidance. But shortly after my mom died, I found a letter she left that validated what I had always sensed.

In the second paragraph, she revealed how talking about what happened would never be a subject she could discuss with me. For my entire life, I kept the disappointment of the failed promise to myself.

Of course, this wasn't the first time I reflected on this part of my past and the ordeal that changed my life forever but reconnecting to the incident gave me a needed perspective. Once again, I recognized how deep my fear of disappointment went and how the cause, seated in childhood, continued to affect me.

With this renewed awareness I had a choice. As an adult, I could decide how this setback in my life impacted me.

The next morning as I made coffee, I felt the familiar dread of heading up to my office to face my computer. As I drank my second cup, I thought about ways I could procrastinate. Do laundry. Wash the dishes. Boil more water for more coffee. But I knew better.

I recognized fear rumbling in the pit of my stomach and the heaviness weighted in my legs making it difficult to get going and I knew why. It had a name. Disappointment was buzzing around. Would I let it continue to thwart my progress? Hell, no. My capable conscious adult told disappointment to take a hike.

Fear is part of me. It breathes, has life. It can overwhelm me, disempower me, and often it fuels my procrastination. But fear is also an attention-getter. A warning system that motivates self-inquiry. Because once I understand what I fear, I can decide if it's time to run, hide, or take action.

When it came to this book, I named the fear that kept my fingers away from the computer. In so doing, fear, as Guidance counseled, did shrink to a size I could live with, and I wrote without stopping day after day.

Reflections

There are plenty of times when knowing the root cause for what's troubling me isn't necessary. Sometimes simply accepting that I'm going through a difficult period is all I need to feel better. But when it comes to fears that stop me, acceptance isn't enough. I don't appreciate a fear that gets the better of me.

Guidance reminds us that fears can loom large, choking the life from us. But a fear that is recognized and named, breaks down into manageable bite-size pieces, that are easier to sink our teeth into and chew.

1. Where do you experience fear in your body?
2. Does naming what you are afraid of change how you deal with the fear?
3. When has fear guided you for the better? When has it thwarted your progress?

Many years ago, a man who owned an antique shop I frequented handed me a paperback copy of *A Return to Love: Reflections on the Principles of a 'Course in Miracles* by Marianne Williamson (HarperCollins, 1992). I don't remember much about that book; except she laid out specific ideas about "fear" and "love" that felt right on target.

Over the years, Guidance added their insights about fear. Their messages brought my understanding to the next level—how fear can affect us both positively and negatively, but it's up to us to differentiate.

I've come to recognize when fear settles within me as if a boa constrictor were tightening my belly, squeezing the life from me. I pay attention. If fear is working against me, I inquire in order to name what I fear. I need to know so I can loosen its hold.

22. Forgiveness

Sweet forgiveness is the answer.

Forgiveness offers an opportunity to transform what is hard, to find the courage to move on, to move through in light—your light. Forgiveness is a task, but you can learn to do it.

Forgiveness does not condone an act. It does not take away what was hurt, but one can move on.

Your willingness to forgive helps others, but more importantly, it helps you. For the person who honors forgiveness can find peace.

Is your heart full of resentment, anger, or harsh words that cannot heal you? Is your heart cold when you think of others? What you do to yourself is far worse than what one can do to another, so healing starts with you.

Forgiveness brings compassion. Forgiveness lifts burdens. Forgive and be free.

Forgiving is a tool to find deeper love.

Forgive yourself first, and then finding it for others will come easier.

Holding onto any feeling that closes you to love hurts you, and in that, others too are hurt. Peace and love want to be your guide. Allow the practice of forgiveness to guide you. To show you how to turn a cold heart into one that is warm with care.

This is a challenging task. But for those who spend time feeling what forgiveness offers, all know how forgiveness can heal

My mom and I had a difficult relationship. We were at odds most of the time. I wasn't a complacent child, so when I questioned her reasoning or defied her rules, I was met with physical punishment or abandonment. She once ignored me for twenty-four hours because I angered her. The next day she sent me to school without the usual brown-bag lunch. I was six.

My mom never apologized for her ill-treatment. Her inability to do so drove me crazy. There were plenty of times, however, when I apologized to get back into her good graces. I resented the hypocrisy, the power imbalance, and in turn, her.

I left home at eighteen, moving from the East Coast to the West to get away. After a few years of being on my own, I tried to talk to my mom on several occasions, hoping we might repair what was broken. In my twenties, I invited her to one of my therapy sessions.

My mom responded matter-of-factly to my hurts . . . that she had done the best she could. Her pat answer made me furious. I viewed her denial as a way she sidestepped responsibility.

Her dismissive attitude fueled my hurt and resentment and alienated us further. I couldn't talk to my mom without feeling how she had done me wrong, and I couldn't visit her without feeling she had never done me right.

I remained a dutiful daughter, however. My sense of obligation, along with my desire for change, made it impossible to cut my mother out of my life.

When I returned to the Bronx, we would visit for about an hour or so or go for dinner with my siblings. But she and I made no effort to spend much time together. Our phone conversations were no better. She talked about the weather or meeting up with her friends while I feigned interest.

I felt like a terrible daughter. I was unable to express real feelings of warmth toward my mom or take in any warmth from her. When she said she loved me, her words bounced off, never reaching my core. I remained aloof.

By my midforties, I was struggling emotionally. This wasn't new for me, but by then, conflict with people at work or with friends was taking its toll.

I prayed for change. Guidance sent a message.

Forgive your mother, and you will be healed.

Although I understood that forgiveness had merit, I was skeptical. Guidance promised to help. They suggested I host a forgiveness circle.

I invited three women I knew whose challenging relationships with their mothers affected their sense of well-being. I told them about my plan. Each woman responded with interest. We all felt overwhelmed about how to go about the task.

Guidance made good on their assurance. Each week, they brought me their wisdom, and in turn, I brought what they told me to the group. Their first message gave us the needed starting point.

What will you try to forgive? You want to forgive your mothers, but you must first learn to forgive yourselves. All of you feel bad that you cannot love your mothers. You carry an inner burden because of your ill-treatment toward your mothers—for not having compassion for them, for not understanding them, for not always knowing who they are—since you feel so misunderstood by them. Forgiving someone else must start with the forgiveness you believe you are due, so forgive yourselves first.

We all agreed we felt like terrible daughters. We also realized how, for most of our entire adult life, the unrelenting guilt and shame we carried festered like a wound poisoning our self-worth. This long-held denial reminded me of times when I left a week's worth of dirty dishes in the sink without making the connection that I would be dealing with the consequences.

Admitting our self-hate, within the safety of the group, was the first step in our healing process. Each of us judged ourselves for how we acted toward our moms, but we agreed to express these feelings without fear of being judged.

Guidance's message rang true. Healing had to begin with us. We decided there would be no victims or perpetrators. We agreed to start with a blank slate. We let go of past perceptions and took a break from beating up ourselves and our moms.

Guidance continued to advise us week after week. We read articles and books about forgiveness that offered encouragement. We looked to others for inspiration—brave, amazing, resilient people who had been able to forgive under unimaginable circumstances, enduring far worse crimes than our mothers had inflicted on us.

For eight weeks, we did rituals and exercises to cast off our guilt and shame until we felt compassion and forgiveness toward ourselves. We kept faith in the idea that our ability to forgive our mothers would eventually happen. For many of us, it did.

I came to understand how my mom was an insecure person, filled with self-ridicule. I recognized the hurt she carried. We were both unhappy in our own skins, and we both caused each other unhappiness.

I felt true compassion for my mom, who was born in 1926, which meant she had fewer outlets than me for self-reflection and support. My sympathy for both of us grew. Perhaps she really had done the best she could.

When the forgiveness group ended, we all gained a new perspective. The group helped me to heal to a degree, but acting in a new way with my mom took longer. I remained guarded when we talked on the phone. Sometimes, I backslid into my defensive posture. I noticed my old patterns with a new vigilance—how lashing out hurt her and hurt me because I felt terrible for doing so.

During this period, I remained hopeful that, as Guidance predicted, my burdened heart could also change. I wanted to heal. It took several more years for that miracle to occur.

I will never forget sitting across the table from my ninety-year-old mother in an Italian restaurant in Manhattan, warmly enjoying her company. A few days earlier, I had flown from Oregon for my annual visit.

In the taxi on my way to meet her, I felt the usual anxiety about spending time together. I imagined our shared history when one of us inevitably said something that pained the other. Even if that didn't happen, there would be awkward silence and then the familiar air of tension between us, so we would skip dessert to get the hell away from each other. Then, I would spend the next twenty-four hours feeling lousy about our time together.

None of what I anticipated happened. To my surprise, I felt at ease. Throughout lunch, we experienced none of the usual stilted conversations as we tried finding something to talk about. I genuinely listened with interest to what she had to say. She returned the favor.

We were having such a good time that when my mom asked if I would meet her again in two days (seeing her in the same week was rare), I eagerly said yes ("eagerly" was also rare). We were on new ground.

Throughout my life, the fury I felt toward my mom intensified because she refused to change. But forgiving myself changed me and brought with it more kindness for myself, my mom, and other people in my life, in ways I never could have predicted.

I remembered bosses who treated me like crap, ex-girlfriends who betrayed me, and friends who criticized me behind my back. The same words my mom used, which once sent me reeling into a tailspin of anger, now fueled my understanding. Perhaps they too were doing the best they could. We all make mistakes, have errors in judgment. and need to be forgiven every now and then.

I never talked to my mom about how I forgave her or myself. I didn't think it was necessary. The results were enough. I softened with her. For my mom's part, she softened too.

I became less defensive. Maybe this caused her to be less cautious around me. I'm not sure. What is certain is that I no longer pretended I cared for her. When she said she loved me, I took in her love and returned a genuine love her way.

I spent most of my life unable to imagine feeling anything but indifference about my mom's passing. Unexpectedly, she died while writing this book. And I, who never thought I would miss anything about her once she was gone, cried at her funeral along with my sister and brother.

What Guidance taught me about forgiveness turned out to be true. Forgiveness is a process that heals the one who can forgive.

Reflections

Our ability to forgive releases our pain. Without forgiveness, we're held back. We are the ones who are stuck. When we forgive, we no longer feel burdened. When we forgive, we can move forward with our lives.

Circumstances that initiate our need to forgive others or ourselves will show up repeatedly throughout our lives. True forgiveness comes when we are humble. This means we learn to let go of blame and guilt. Forgiveness takes practice.

1. How does it feel to be forgiven? How does it feel when someone won't forgive you?
2. How easy or difficult is it to apologize to someone?
3. What are you willing to do in order to forgive? Is there anything that could stop you from forgiving?

There was a time when my inability to wrap my head around forgiveness was as impossible a task as comprehending the one hundred thousand million stars in the galaxy. My mind can't grasp the enormity of the star-galaxies thing; I'm good with that. It's not something I feel the need to change about myself.

With that said, perhaps you too are okay with certain things about you that don't need to change. But if being unable to forgive is on that list, I highly recommend you scratch it off. Make forgiveness a priority. Learn how to forgive. This enlightened practice opened my heart. It is a true wake-up call to love.

23. Loss

Loss is what brings you closer to the Universe's grace.

Every day there are losses and all humans experience loss. Loss is a mark of time. For no matter what is lost, once gone, it serves as a reminder of how loss comes and goes in your life.

Loss is a memory of emptiness.

Emptiness is not still, so loss is like a wave that comes to shore, spent. All its energy heads back toward the ocean, docile and calm, only to become again what it must—a new wave crashing on land. That cycle of the wave is the death cycle, loss played out over and over, for energy is not stagnant. There is nothing that keeps energy still.

Make room to allow what can never be permanent and see with your own eyes what you will experience in your life, over and over.

Your soul cries out for this reminder of what loss brings. Allow for that space to heal and wash over you.

I was nine when I had surgery on my fully functioning shorter leg that left it marred with scars, painful nerve damage, and limited mobility, which to this day severely hampers my ability to walk.

I have never known a cure for the pain of that loss. I doubt there is one. But I believe what Guidance says about loss: to allow for it to come and accept it on its terms.

Some years ago, I found the courage to reflect on the positive perspective of what the loss of my leg's mobility offered my life. This wasn't an easy undertaking, yet I allowed my mind to wander, to go where it wanted.

I was back in college obtaining my degree in Therapeutic Recreation, which required a certain number of volunteer hours with a variety of social service agencies. I signed up with a Suicide Prevention hotline.

I sat through weeks of training before I could take calls. On our last night of class, the facilitator asked that we make a list of ten relatives and friends who were important to us. When we were finished, he directed us to pick one person to cross off the list. That person would be gone from our lives forever.

The task felt impossible. We had no choice. I put a line through my grandmother. I loved her dearly and would miss her terribly, but she was in her nineties by then, so I knew she might be gone from my life at any moment.

Then he had us cross off another person, then another. We did this repeatedly until our losses mounted and there were no more loved ones left on the page.

There was no discussion other than acknowledging the heavy-heartedness that lingered in the room. We were left to sort out our feelings on our own.

As I stood from my chair to leave, a classmate asked for a ride home. When he got in my car, he told me the exercise upset him. Up to that moment, he hadn't thought about what it would be like to see his parents die or no longer have his brothers in his life.

He said he felt depressed. As he talked, I noticed I didn't feel the same. The exercise had been difficult, but it was over. I was heading home. I wasn't depressed or upset.

I asked him if he had ever experienced a tragic loss. He said no.

I couldn't relate to his answer. Wasn't loss an inevitable part of life? I felt smug. How had he not experienced loss up to now? In that moment, I felt worldly, years older even though we were both in our midtwenties. But secretly, I wondered about being so cavalier.

To this day, when I'm overcome by the initial gut-wrenching pang that loss brings, I rarely allow myself to linger there. From the ring given to me by my grandparents that was stolen to a new pain searing my foot, I acknowledge what's happening, then push on past, taking the loss in stride.

I feel a certain righteousness having this perspective, but I also judge my reaction as it differs from the distress I see in others. I harshly compare myself to how others react, as I did that night with my passenger and another time in high school while riding the subway with a friend.

We were both holding onto the middle pole for balance as the train car rocked back and forth. When the doors opened at our stop, I noticed my bracelet was gone.

As we walked onto the subway platform, my friend became unglued when I told her. She grew increasingly upset. She went on about how we should have stayed on the train to look for my bracelet.

I had already moved on, not giving the loss a second thought. I remember wondering if her response was the correct one. If breezing through the loss meant something was wrong with me.

Guidance's prompt to look at what my experience with loss offered me, brought a fresh perspective. I finally found the grace instead of what had long troubled me.

On mornings when I stumble out of bed with a knee so stiff, I can barely walk, I don't allow this loss of mobility to define my mood. I don't allow myself to get emotionally discombobulated. I get up. I keep going. I don't dwell. I like this about myself.

Due to my disability, I have had years of practice learning to be resilient to loss. When I think of the many ways my emotions are triggered—how they often overtake and overwhelm me—I am grateful that loss is at least one I manage to remain clear-headed about.

The many names I crossed off my list that evening in the Suicide Prevention class have predictably left my life, including loved ones who weren't on the list—a cherished cousin, aunts, uncles, and more than one adored friend.

When my dad died a few years ago, losing him hit me with the type of grief that brought me to my knees. Yet thankfully, my lifelong experience with loss kept me afloat through my tears.

I believe what Guidance says—that loss is inescapable. Of course, that doesn't mean I'm prepared for all the emotional upheaval that loss can bring, as I learned with the death of my dad, but I'm equipped to handle the ride. I am proud of my resilience due to what I learned early in life. Being expectant of loss's consistent nature spares me from being surprised by its ever-persistent existence.

Reflections

Loss is our common reality—not only in our lives but one reflected in nature. Guidance points out that loss resonates in our souls—that place where we are most vulnerable but also might feel unencumbered.

If we thought about loss like a blank canvas, this would increase our ability to let go of expectations. We might feel easier about the unknown and what comes next. We could get better at living with the unexpected detours that loss brings.

1. How do you cope with loss?
2. What have you positively gained by experiencing loss?
3. Would accepting the inevitability of loss change anything about the way you live?

None of us have a choice about when or how loss enters our life. Therefore, we truly can't know how we'll react to it. We can, however, be mindful that experiencing loss is part of life. And perhaps, in this way, we might better accept the little losses that come our way, like my bracelet, for instance, that might prepare us for the bigger losses.

24. Sadness and Sorrow

*Sadness and sorrow are what you
feel because you are human.*

Know only that your sadness and sorrow are formed because you know love.
Because you know compassion.
Because you are human.
We applaud this, and you should too.

In 2004, a massive tsunami in the Indian Ocean took the lives of two hundred and thirty thousand people in fourteen countries. Innocent people, many locals, and many tourists enjoying life on a sunny morning were swept away by the sea. So many lives lost in a flash of minutes meant an unfathomable amount of sorrow that surviving relatives and loved ones had to bear.

The sheer number who died suddenly and without warning remains astronomical. At that time, I felt the impact of the sadness emanating from continents around the globe. I wondered about the victims of the devastation—those who were caught off guard with no way to escape.

All of it troubled me—the loss, the grief, the sadness, and my own fears about death—so I went to the altar in my home to talk to Guidance.

Death comes as it comes for all.

Of course, I heard this from them before, but this time their matter-of-fact answer caught me off guard. What they said sounded so cold. Guidance usually wrapped their message with care and yet I couldn't deny that their response carried an undeniable truth.

I conceded that their simple reminder about the experience of dying in unexpected or sudden ways wasn't born out of callousness; it was honest. Although I recognized the sincerity of their message, it didn't stop me from thinking about the hundreds of thousands of people in Thailand and elsewhere around the world left struggling with a deep sorrow I found unimaginable because so many of their loved ones were gone forever.

I went to Guidance again to push for another answer, one that would make sense of so many people suffering such an insurmountable amount of sadness.

Those who are sad and filled with sorrow do so because they loved so greatly. Love is what all who suffer this sadness have in common. Sadness is not the only thing they know. They also know love, and therein lies the gift.

Guidance's words came as I stood in front of the maple altar my carpenter husband built. This sacred wooden object is small, just under two feet high, and about eight inches wide. He had lined the back wall with soft cedar, where I tacked a postcard from a dear friend and mentor that read, "What we resist persists." A reminder at that moment to let go.

On the altar's bottom shelf sits a small black ceramic bowl filled with the tiny stones and seashells Johnny gifted me from his long, solitary beach walks. I lifted the bowl and took in the scent of its contents. The faint hint of seaweed and salt still present.

I picked up one of the smaller shells, feeling the smoothness of its shiny white interior contrasted with the rough ridges covered in brown freckled spots on the other side. As I turned the shell over in my hand, the sadness I felt for those swept into the sea mixed with a peaceful resolution. I cried, overcome by the purity of love's grace emanating from so many, for so many who were no longer here.

Reflections

What brings each of us sorrow and sadness is personal, yet these feelings are as pure in expression as laughter and joy. Admittedly, I hate feeling sad. But there are times when my sorrow is so deep and poignant that the emotion is impossible to ignore.

1. How do you respond when others are sad?
2. How do you like to be treated by others when you are filled with sorrow?
3. How do you treat yourself when you are overcome with sadness?

If awareness is all and perspective is mutable, we can find comfort knowing that sadness and sorrow are expressions born from how much we care.

25. Shame

Shame is a suffering sickness.

Shame is a cloak that humans must learn to remove.

For in the wilds of life, shame is a creature that has no place. Shame won't protect you. It will only serve to harm you more. Harmful in its wrath, it will bury you until there is no more of you.

Life is mysterious.

Life is free.

Life is joy.

If joy is not your mantra, check to see if shame weighs you down. For nothing in you is shameful. If there is a hint of shame, know that shame must not be carried.

Transform shame. Forgive self so you know compassion toward self. This will alleviate shame and make you whole.

Whole is your birthright. Whole is you; alive, joyous, and free. Peace be with you without shame. We love you.

On a dreary, cold, cloudy day in December, an ambulance transported me home from a six-month stay in the hospital. I arrived in the full body cast I had worn for the past few months. It wrapped around my torso, stopping right below my breasts, continuing down my right leg above the knee, and covering my entire left leg down to the tips of my toes.

Both legs were spread apart by a wooden bar that held them in a wide fixed *V* position. A hole had been cut at just the right spot, enabling me to release all my business into a bedpan. For the next six months, I would live like this.

My dad concocted a stretcher bed out of plywood and old baby carriage wheels so I could roll from the living room, which was now my bedroom, to the dining room. These were the only two rooms in our house I could access.

Stuck at home required homeschooling for fourth grade. Without the opportunity to make new friends, my mom invited past classmates from third grade to celebrate my tenth birthday.

Nina and I hadn't been in touch since the previous June when I entered the hospital. Up to that point, we spent many weekends and even some weekday afternoons in one of our bedrooms, playing with Barbie dolls and chasing each other while laughing and being silly. I can still summon the eagerness I felt back then as I anticipated seeing her again.

I was marooned on the stretcher bed like a beached whale when my friends arrived. One by one, each girl said hello, then disappeared upstairs to the second floor to play in the bedroom I had previously shared with my sister. I spent the afternoon alone, listening to the giggles and commotion coming from the floor above until my mom called everyone down for cake.

As my dad wheeled me into the dining room, I saw Nina for the first time. She must have passed me at some point without my noticing. As the glow of birthday candles came toward me, I watched Nina across the table.

Now, as an adult, I suspect she might have been scared of me. After all, before the hospital, I ran, jumped, and did all the things she could. I can only imagine how shocking it must have been to see me unrecognizable, dressed in white plaster.

But, at my birthday party, I didn't have this understanding. Back then, my response to Nina and the other girls was to retreat into myself. I thought I deserved their unkindness.

My memory of what happened after I blew out the candles remains fuzzy. I don't remember if I ate a slice of birthday cake or if I opened gifts. Did I even receive gifts?

What I do remember is being back in the living room watching Nina at the front door putting on her coat. Her mom pointed my way. Nina bounced over, stood by my side, said a quick "goodbye," and left. I never saw her again.

I didn't speak up for myself that day. There was no self-righteous anger or display of hurt feelings. No show of disappointment, nor asking for something to be different. I was silent and compliant. This is what shame brings.

Once I could finally move through the world again, I wore a leg brace and walked with a visible limp while using crutches. Children stared. Adults whispered, trying not to look. I endured the humiliation as I had with the girls at my birthday party. I saw myself the way I imagined others did; a freak, a circus sideshow, and therefore someone who should expect to be maligned.

Shame made me polite and submissive. When a stranger asked "what's wrong with you," or "why are you limping," I answered their prying obediently as if I owed them an explanation.

It never occurred to me that I could tell them to mind their own business. Instead, I recited the entire true story. I laid out being born with one leg shorter and how, through surgeries, my disability worsened.

What I divulged left me feeling vulnerable, powerless, and more embarrassed. Their curiosity served to reinforce how different I felt.

As I think about this now, I know that I had every right to feel proud and courageous for having endured so much at a young age. But back then, I never gave myself permission to reflect in that way.

Instead, I swallowed shame willingly for most of my life until healing came. Guidance reminded me that I had the power to believe or reject how others defined me, and certainly, I had the power to define how I wanted to view myself. Shame is in the eye of the beholder.

Once this beholder became conscious of how shame infiltrated my life, I questioned why I would want to remain its victim. Shame made me feel shitty, and that shitty, self-apologetic feeling is one I chose to cast aside.

Today, when someone I don't know inquires about my limp, I respond without the long explanation that used to be my default. Instead, I answer with a matter-of-fact attitude, responding with confident honesty instead of the shameful stance that once held me back. I tell them without a hint of apology; that the limp is the way I walk. That this is who I am. That this is who I have always been.

Reflections

Shame dismantled my pride, confidence, and sense of worthiness. That's what shame does. Shame is an internalized oppressor. We often remain unaware that shame is calling the shots instead of remembering that shame shouldn't be allowed to have so much influence.

If you're looking to find ways to break a cycle of shame, contemplating these questions might help.

1. Can you identify the ways that shame holds you back from accepting yourself?
2. What might change if feeling shame were lessened or healed?

Shame is physically, emotionally, and spiritually abusive. Feeling shame adds stress to our lives as we absorb its hellish infringement on our happiness. As Guidance points out, shame holds us back from self-love.

When I realized how shame affected me, I knew Guidance was right. Shame didn't allow for loving myself. This made me sad. Releasing shame came with a flood of tears.

All of our experiences contribute to who we are. So, yes, even shame informs our life, but it shouldn't have the ability to take the heart of who we are away.

26. Time

Use time as you see fit. Time does not use you.

WHEEL of FORTUNE.

Imagine how time is man-made and has no real purpose. Imagine that time is not an entity of control.

Turn your face away from the watch-keeper—the timepiece, the clock, the thing that "watches" you—that keeps you trapped and strapped.

Watch your own concept of time change from day to day and from moment to moment. Ten minutes can feel like an hour or sixty seconds, does it not? In that understanding, you must then see how time can be played with.

Time is a capsule surrounded by what is infinite. Infinity is always at your disposal because it encompasses all. And within all, infinity is life, breath, and love.

Play with time. It can be stretched or slowed. Infinity is your friend.

As an administrative assistant for a large urban community center, my duties included working with the public. I also supported a staff of six and managed many of the center's daily financial requirements like paying bills and forking over petty cash.

I didn't have my own office, so I couldn't shut a door with a "do not disturb" sign. I sat a few feet from the front doors, in full view, which meant I had to be available to whoever walked in and deal with whatever took place. My eight-hour day never felt long enough.

When an unexpected project came my way, I squeezed the assignment in between all my other duties. Picture one of those cartoon octopuses with eight arms moving in every direction, simultaneously, and you might have a sense of my daily existence.

One afternoon, after lunch, my boss approached my workstation holding a legal pad with handwritten notes she needed typed. I had already crammed what felt like six hours of work into my four-hour morning. When I looked up at the large clock in the lobby, it was one o'clock. My boss needed the document by three.

I felt the familiar squeeze of time. In light of everything I had to do, plus the countless interruptions from walk-ins and phone calls, I knew two hours was pushing it.

To cope, I filed faster. I hurried customers off the phone. I quickened my pace, hoping to free up the time needed to complete the looming task I hadn't started.

When I looked at the clock, another half hour had passed. My mouth was dry. My heart raced. I stood at my desk, letting a phone call go to voice mail.

I recognized the tension, the pressure. I had been here before—overwhelmed, rushing around as if I had taken amphetamines. I had had enough.

With nothing to lose, I told the Universe I needed time to slow down. The experiment would succeed or not. I gave into trust, but I was skeptical.

After setting my intention, I sat down in front of the computer. I slowed my breath. I stopped hurrying. I answered phone calls with ease. I dealt with the usual interruptions but didn't lose my composure. I refused to give in to what Guidance called, the "watch-keeper."

After a while, I settled into a comfortable typing rhythm, a nice cruising speed. I didn't look at the clock again until I pulled the final edited copy out of the printer.

It was two-fifty. I had ten minutes to spare. I was dumb-founded.

The next time I played with time happened to be the morning I slept through my alarm. I woke in a stupor. I jumped out of bed as if bitten by a bee. I rushed into the bathroom to take a quick shower.

I told the Universe that I had to be out of the house by eight-twenty, with enough time to drive to work and get to my desk. As before, I refused to panic, and I stopped paying attention to the clock.

As the water sprayed over me, I felt my hair. It needed washing. This took longer. I had a moment of doubt, but the rebel in me wanted to test time. I wanted to see how far I could push the experiment that morning. I lathered up.

By the time I buttoned my coat to leave for work, my hair was dry, my lunch had been made, and my dog was chewing on her cookie after having done her business outside. All that and I wasn't going to be late.

Time and I were getting along. I wondered if this had always been true to some extent. Weren't there mornings when I forgot to set an alarm but woke up at the exact moment I needed?

Perhaps time and I were already cohorts with one another. The only difference is that I took our relationship for granted. But how does time shift to suit my needs?

I imagine there could be a scientific connection, although if there is one, it is likely to go over my head. Unlike time, science and I are not in sync. I do have a theory, however, as to what might be happening.

According to Guidance, limiting beliefs can create limited results. For example, if I expect a negative outcome, I often end up with a negative result. Why wouldn't this be true about time? If I'm anxious about time, wouldn't it make sense that time might reflect this back and be anxious with me?

If you believe, as I do, that our thoughts have sway, then it's possible that when we panic about lacking enough time to finish a task, it becomes harder to complete it on schedule. For example, when we're late for an appointment, perhaps it's because, even before we leave the house, we're convinced we won't make it there in time.

One day I had fifteen minutes to finish a bank transaction, get back in my car, and drive crosstown to attend a qigong class. The long bank line meant I would probably be late.

As I thought about leaving, I decided, once again, to trust Guidance's teachings about time. I breathed deeply. This released my stress. With a clearer head, I told the Universe while convincing myself, that time had to slow down. And it did. I strolled into class with a minute to spare.

I'm not saying I have complete control over what I'm able to manifest due to how I think. But I do have a choice about what I think and how I react. When it comes to time, I can believe this tool to be the authority, or that it has no real validity.

When I mentioned this to a friend, she reminded me that she, too, received a message about time from Guidance some years back when she came for a reading. Their advice was to ask the Universe for "more time" whenever she felt pressed. This has worked for her.

Whether you choose to ask for more time or for time to slow down or for a specific amount of time doesn't seem to matter. When we play with time, regardless of the technique, we are agreeing with the notion that "time is on our side."

If nothing else, handing my boss her document ten minutes early, washing my hair even though it takes longer, and leaving the bank with time to spare, has offered direct, concrete, down-to-earth feedback that stretches my limited perceptions about time.

Each outcome with its unexpected gifts has made me a truer champion of time being malleable. The mystery continues. But casting out logic is what brought Tarot into my life, and believing in experiences I can't logically explain is why Guidance continues to visit.

Reflections

As a practice, working with time's flexibility has the potential to fortify your acceptance of life's mysterious ways. The next time you believe that time is against you, why not ask the Universe for help? Remember, we are the ones treating time as the enemy so we can decide to be friends instead.

1. How do you feel and react when you are pressured by time?
2. How do you talk about time? For example, do you ever tell yourself that you don't have enough time?
3. How does your perception of time influence your decisions and mood?

Many of us have discovered that our emotions are tied to the timekeeping clock. Sometimes we feel stressed. At other times, we feel relief.

Gaining awareness about how time truly affects you is a good reason to experiment with it. But no matter your motivation, I hope you discover as I did, that playing with time, at its most basic, is a fun thing to do.

27. Faith

When you need faith most, is when most lose faith.

You, who are so alive with the idea of help from the Universe, from God, from angels, from ancestors, or from a spirit you may not see but believe in, must know, then, how to keep faith.

One lives with faith when one lives with the knowledge of help.

If you need help, faith is your best friend. Faith is always there so all we ask is that you reach for it. All you must do is tap into it and, in so doing, faith cannot be lost.

Faith makes you stronger.

Faith gives you courage.

Faith is pure.

Faith is not a thought. Faith is a feeling that connects you to the greater Universe, and to others, so you know you are not alone, so you know you are part of the whole.

But faith also guides you to your best self. What you discover when you grab the hand of faith is a stronger belief in you.

Faith offers a way back to you, a sense of knowing you are on the right path. For when you have faith, you can get through when you are unsure or feel lost.

Faith is the belief in your life, which is the greatest life of all. And in this, the greatest gift of faith is having faith in yourself.

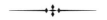

A while back, I began to toy with the idea of making oracle cards based on Guidance's wisdom. I'm not short on ideas. The execution of those ideas, however, is where I get stuck.

Other than writing down the messages I received from Guidance, I didn't know how to produce cards or find an artist to create the graphics.

The good news, however, is that I have faith which means I can let go of the particulars while trusting that the Universe will point me in the best-suited direction. When I walk with faith, I do so without expectations. I don't need to have all the answers or know how it will work out. I let go of the timelines and trust deeply that what is meant to be will show itself. This doesn't mean I sit on my hands and do nothing, but I don't give in to worrying about the details.

I happened to be on the phone with my brother when I thought to ask his advice. Daniel has an artistic eye, so I questioned him about the type of artist to pursue. He suggested someone well-versed in textile design. Textile designers work with patterns and repetition, exactly the type of graphics I envisioned for the cards.

Our conversation gave me the information I needed but two years later, the project was no further along. I met artists during that time, but none were right. The project simmered on the back burner while I pursued other ideas.

One was to offer Tarot Guidance readings at the Saturday Market in Eugene, the longest-running outdoor crafts fair in the United States. On my first day, I stood alone, with a hot cup of coffee to warm me from the early morning chill. In Eugene, May can be overcast, cold, and rainy, especially in the early hours of the day. As expected, it was sweater-and-scarf weather.

I was bundled up, along with about two hundred other vendors. Everyone appeared friendly but seemed to know the ropes and each other with a familiarity I lacked. As a newcomer, I felt a bit intimidated.

While I waited to be assigned to a booth space, I saw a woman wearing a colorful tunic. I wanted to tell her how much I admired her outfit, but I felt shy.

Despite my awkwardness, I found the courage to open my mouth. Sandra was appreciative of my compliment, and we struck up a conversation. I learned she was a first-time vendor like me. We formed a bond of support as we waited for our names to be called.

Two hours later, the first person walked into my booth to request a reading. I knew Ann. She mentioned she ran into a friend who told her my booth location among the maze of sellers that stretched for two square city blocks. I was shocked to hear that a vendor knew me, let alone the location of my booth. Ann explained that her friend was Sandra, the only person I talked to that entire morning.

Sandra never made it back to the market after that first day, but soon after, she emailed to ask if I wanted to meet at a local coffee shop. I happily agreed.

We talked for over an hour, enjoying each other's company. As I stood up to leave, Sandra pulled out her phone to show me pictures of the textile swatches she had designed.

I knew Sandra sewed. I saw her beautiful custom prayer flags and buntings at the market, but I had yet to learn that she created artwork for fabric. She scrolled through the shapes and forms imprinted with spirals, circles, and other playful symbols in bold, rich colors.

Sandra's aesthetic felt right for the cards, but I hesitated to ask for her help. I barely knew her. Despite my reservation, I couldn't contain my excitement. I mentioned the project.

Without hesitation, Sandra shared many ideas, including font styles that I had yet to consider. She was intrigued and agreed to think about it.

Some might say I found Sandra solely based on my patience, but they would be wrong. If it had only been patience supporting my resolve during those two years, frustration would have surely kicked in while I wondered obsessively about finding a suitable artist. Patience would have taken emotional effort on my part. Working with faith feels effortless.

With faith, I don't have to be in the driver's seat. The only requirement is that I keep the idea alive, believe in its merits, and then pay attention. This is what faith asks me to do.

With faith, I can accept periods when I don't have answers or don't know how to reach a desired goal. Faith allows me to relax while I wait.

This connection to what's possible is an invitation. If I do my part, then there's a chance the Universe can do its part, perhaps show me something I didn't know or surprise me—like finding out that Sandra designed fabric art. This also means I often place my faith in the Universe's timeline instead of my own.

Although some might view using faith to find an artist as a frivolous example of this spiritual ideal, I would disagree. Sure, faith is there for the big-ticket items, like when I had breast cancer. But it also allows me to keep my cool for the smallest of life's hiccups and challenges, like when I'm searching for a parking spot at Costco.

Merriam-Webster defines "faith" as a "firm belief in something for which there is no proof." Certainly, I can't prove what faith is. What I can do, however, is continue to have firsthand experiences that increase my belief.

This is not to say that my faith never wavers. When I'm struggling in life, my confidence in this unseen source can come into question. Will I ditch faith when I need its constancy the most?

But then, an image comes. I am stuck on a slippery, jagged rock covered with moss in the middle of a rushing river. I teeter precariously while the whooshing, relentless sound of water drowns out all my senses. I'm overcome by terror, certain that I'll lose my balance and be swept away.

As cold water splashes up around me, faith takes my hand. I spontaneously stand up straighter. I stop trembling as I'm gently guided, walking with sureness on stone after wobbly stone until I'm on the other side—safe, with my feet firmly planted on solid, dry land.

Reflections

Keeping faith means I trust the Universe's benevolence. Does this mean it's all going to work out for me? Perhaps. But there's no certainty.

With faith, I believe that whatever happens is meant to be. This calm state is one of faith's great gifts.

If you haven't yet contemplated how faith influences your life, perhaps these questions will help you to clarify your connection.

1. What does faith mean to you?
2. How does faith inform your life? Or does it?
3. Have you ever ditched faith depending on which way the wind was blowing? And if so, what did you learn by letting faith go?

I have experienced periods of self-hate so consuming that I could see no clear way past that feeling. During those times, I wanted to give up on life. On one particularly bad evening, while I took a warm bath, I desperately asked Guidance for the strength to get through. They told me to have faith.

With this reminder I felt a soft cushion keeping me afloat. Faith settled through me. I knew I would survive the demons attacking my mind. I felt assured that my self-loathing was temporary. This optimistic perspective is what faith offers, along with a buoyed feeling of support that I believe is available to us all.

28. Suffering

A comradery built on suffering
won't help to alleviate suffering.

Your belief in the need to suffer is what keeps suffering alive. So, we tell you this: suffering is not an acceptable destination. But as long as humans believe in suffering, then you can learn from suffering so that it can end in your world.

Joy is the truth, but humans are out of practice with joy's essence. It is not hard to live in joy; it is only hard to believe in the joy that is always there. But that is your path . . . to know that joy is the heart and soul of your existence. Joy is what you truly seek.

If you place your hand on a hot stove, your suffering will not allow you to stay there very long. You don't want to feel pain, yet as humans, you can remain unaware of the tremendous emotional pain you endure.

It is only when you "notice" how you suffer that it can change.

Feel in your body how suffering calls you and undermines you, erases your faith, takes hope away, and creates more pain.

What misery does to you—to your body, mind, and soul—to realize this is the true way to end suffering in every moment.

Noticing your pain will teach you to love.

Noticing your pain brings compassion for yourself and for others.

Noticing your suffering will help you to understand what suffering causes.

The ease of your harmonious nature is as true as the suffering you cause self.

When suffering comes to you, ask for its beauty. Misery can switch to joy, transforming you and transforming the world around you.

For many years—too many to count—I woke up each morning with the weight of suffering so heavily upon me that I couldn't think of one reason to get out of bed. It seemed like a gray cast hung permanently around the periphery of my vision—as if a filter blocked light from entering my eyes even when the sun shone brightly.

I sought traditional therapy. I told my counselor I felt depressed. I never woke to a new day with a light heart. This went on for years. Therapy didn't help.

Later, I sought Guidance's advice. I knew about antidepressants, so I asked if I should take some medication. They told me that I would find another way.

Their answer was a relief. I hate taking pills. If you open my medicine cabinet, you'll only find one single bottle of generic ibuprofen for those rare days when a headache won't quit.

During this soul-searching period, on one particularly bad morning, I couldn't turn off the barrage of negative, internal, self-chastising voices in my head. The chatter continued even as I walked my dog down to the meadow near my house.

I took Bow off her leash. The sweet smell from a recent mowing had her sniffing around the grass while I wandered alone. The crushing self-doubt stayed with me, relentlessly circling my brain like tumbleweed tossing about.

Lost in my own world, I paid no attention to where I stepped until my right shoe made contact with a mound of shit. As I lifted my foot, the disgusting whiff of dog excrement hit my nose. I laughed uncontrollably. I could only have missed the message if I had been in a coma.

As I wiped my sole clean on a patch of grass, I cleansed my mind of all the oppressive self-talk. I walked Bow back home without the pile of crap I had been giving myself all morning.

At home, after Bow settled in and I ate breakfast, I stood at my altar, planning to thank Guidance and the larger Universe for their helpful message. But upon closing my eyes, an unexpected image emerged. I saw gray-silhouetted backs of strangers from the waist up with no distinguishing features.

Startled, I opened my eyes, then shut them as quickly, deciding to allow the vision to continue. The monochromatic blobs bobbed up and down, reminding me of the floating rubber ducks my niece used to play with in her bath when she was a toddler.

The figures were crowded together, huddled in tight rows and as colorless as the world they inhabited. To my horror, I was wedged among them. Trapped. Consumed by misery, along with everyone else. My life sucked. My suffering endless.

I looked upward to catch my breath. To find space. To alleviate the claustrophobia. A thin white line caught my eye. It separated this underworld from an area that looked bright and sunny. I sensed its cheery promise and, with that, an overwhelming possibility that the extreme bleakness wasn't my only option.

I separated from the group. I floated. My desire to cross over and escape the oppressive pit carried me upward.

I hadn't gone far when thousands of arms grabbed my legs, trying to pull me back. They pleaded that I stay with them.

The old saying "misery loves company" was never clearer to me than at that moment. I ignored their request. I soared above the pack. I broke free.

I flew away from the crowd, alone, on my own. Then, I froze in mid-air, stuck, hovering between what I knew and the unfamiliar place that beckoned me. I had doubts about leaving.

How could I abandon the group? My suffering was so intertwined with theirs. I felt guilty for separating myself. Guidance's voice came through.

If you stay, you cannot help them. Misery cannot help misery. Only those who are free of suffering can help others who are consumed by it.

Their words shot me airborne. I became as light as a leaf, twirling effortlessly on the current of a gentle breeze. I sailed skyward, farther away from the restriction of those who beckoned me to stay. I crossed the line, welcomed by the brilliance of an azure blue sky.

With room to move, I danced. Grateful for the space, I made large sweeping gestures with my arms and legs. I took in the smell of citrus and sweet jasmine, realizing how I held my breath in the world below to avoid the rotten stench of decay.

I looked down. I gestured to those beneath me to come, to follow. I begged them to join me. They shook their heads. I understood their hesitation. I, too, had given into suffering, but it no longer suited my well-being.

With Guidance's words ringing in my ears, I knew that staying would have been of little use to them. As tears welled within me, my heart melted as I gained a deeper compassion for myself and for those who would not leave.

Guidance's message about suffering piqued my curiosity about its results and value. Suffering seems to be unavoidable, but now I notice whenever it wears me down.

I no longer wish to endure the enormity of a feeling that brings me to my knees, nor do I want to exacerbate the feeling or prolong its hold on me. Pulling myself away from suffering is about the choice to do so. That choice has grown with time.

Thankfully, the vision I saw at my altar remains. It surfaces when I feel the familiar, oppressive physical feeling that suffering causes.

I recognize once again how my body is constricted. My arms are folded inward. My stomach is tight. These suffocating sensations are oppressive. The opposite of feeling expansive, with my arms wide, my chest open with plenty of room to breathe.

This awareness shines a spotlight on the suffering I inflict on myself. In those moments, I choose again to stop harming myself further. Remaining stuck in a pit of hell is no longer tenable.

Reflections

During my vision, I felt my suffering entwined with everybody else's, and for the first time, perhaps, I felt true compassion. This feeling has remained. I believe Guidance is right. They remind us that as long as we continue to suffer, perhaps we can learn and even gain from the experience.

1. How does suffering affect you physically?
2. What does suffering take from you? What does it offer?
3. How might you experience suffering differently if you noticed how long (days, weeks, months) you held onto suffering?

Sometimes our suffering is brought on by a circumstance, or a person, or we bring it upon ourselves. For the most part, we survive our moments of suffering again and again.

But Guidance makes us aware that if someone pinched our arm hard, within seconds, the physical pain would force us to brush their hand aside and tell them to stop. And yet, too many times we prolong our own suffering.

We don't think to give ourselves permission to stop our emotional pain. Our suffering drags on, and often intensifies as we berate ourselves, as I did that morning in the meadow.

We may not be able to change circumstances that cause us to suffer, but conscious awareness offers us a choice about how long and to what degree we allow our suffering to continue.

29. Joy

Joy is your sanctuary.

Joy was always meant to be where you started and where you'll end.

But humans are funny in their disregard for its source and its abilities.

Joy is your birthplace for hope, peace, acceptance, and livability.

Joy's uplifting presence is made visible in you, by you, and for you. It is available. It doesn't have to be sought. It is always there, here, and around you.

Joy is with you, in your heart, your cells, your light, your loves, your pain, your freedom, your scars, your challenges, and your luminescence.

Joy is made visible in you by just allowing it to be. To allow joy to be, one must remember that it was always your birthright.

Joy is your gift.

Joy is what you are.

Joy is you.

Accept that joy is the truth of your being. There is no greater truth, for joy awakens all lost souls.

Joy awakens all of what lives inside of you. Joy awakens what is known only to you—that you are wise beyond what you know, that you are wise beyond what you perceive as your limitations, and that you are wise to all of who you are.

Joy emanates from you. Make no mistake about this—the challenges you face may diminish the joy you feel, but they cannot eradicate the joy you possess.

Grab joy like you would the brass ring on a merry-go-round. It is your ease, and you have it whenever you are aware of its ever-solid and infinite presence.

When it became apparent that my ever-increasing stress level was negatively affecting my health, I committed to a six-month mindful meditation course. Two months prior, I received a diagnosis of Polymyalgia Rheumatica, a fancy medical term for high inflammation brought on by high stress.

On a scale of one to ten, my pain level reached a twelve. I hoped the many months of meditating in a community, with support, would help turn my condition around.

At the first class, I arrived eager but nervous—my usual state in a new situation with people I don't know. There were three women already seated. I found a comfortable spot on one of the two couches that faced each other. I pulled out a pen and my journal, which we were asked to bring, and listened silently to our facilitator as she explained what we would be learning during the six-month course.

When she finished, she asked each of us to express, in a few words, what we hoped to gain from our time together. I expected to say "stress relief." To my surprise, I blurted "joy."

I identified as a somber person. Not negative per se, but someone whose thoughts are laced with seriousness—as if it's up to me to stay sane and rational while everyone else cuts loose to have fun. While others are kidding around, I'm observing. When something funny is said, I'm on a delay, two or three beats behind before I laugh.

When my friend Joan mentioned how she cracked herself up while doing chores around her house, I only wished that I could make myself laugh too. I wanted to be easy-going. Able to kick back, feel the light-heartedness of joy.

Once class was in full swing, I meditated daily. I focused my intention on why I couldn't perceive joy. I searched for an answer, a reason, with little results.

On one particular evening, during our usual check-in when we shared insights about our meditation practice, I told the group, as I had each week, that I still didn't feel joy.

The facilitator turned my way. She looked at me as if she had been waiting for the right moment, or maybe a sign that I was ready to hear what she had to tell me. Gently, she mentioned that "joy" was around all of us all the time.

Her statement acted like a reboot to my system, as if each cell realigned with the truth of her words and what Guidance had also been trying to help me to understand; that feeling of joy rested on my belief in its infinite availability.

The next time I meditated, I asked Guidance to help me discover the joy that existed in the larger realm. They offered a simple response.

Reach to joy.

I resettled in my chair and did what Guidance suggested. With my eyes closed, I focused on my breath. It didn't take long before my consciousness extended outside the rigid confines of my body, expanding my senses past my studio walls that seemed to disappear.

I fixated on the comforting darkness behind my eyes, afraid that if I opened them, the experience would be ruined. With the walls of my studio gone, I traveled beyond the outer reaches into an infinite state that suggested nothingness and everything. Then beyond. Unencumbered light emanated from within me and outside of me. Engulfed in this pure essence, Guidance's words and the facilitator's counsel proved true.

I felt joy's presence. As I sat, a feeling of unrestrained contentment, connected to all life and all humanity settled within me. I smiled, without expecting to or trying to, or thinking about how.

Then I heard a voice, from the deepest of knowing places. *You know joy. You are joy. You have always been joy.*

For too long, I believed in joy's elusive quality. On days when I didn't wake up energetic, welcoming of the day, or the many times I missed the punchline of a joke, I thought joy didn't exist because I defined it based on a limited view of myself.

It struck me that I had been so fixated on what joy *wasn't* that I hadn't noticed what joy *was*.

My ignorance reminded me of being a little girl who didn't see the moon until my dad told me to look up. Now joy, like the moon, was recognizable, and I lived on a new planet.

Joy was uncomplicated and easily accessed. I felt joy when I sat on the couch next to Johnny or relaxed in the company of a trusted friend. Joy held me when I played hand drums or sat among tall trees or ate french fries.

And when I connect to my breath, I bask in the simplicity of acknowledging that I am here, on this earth, and that being alive is joy.

I shook my head at the absurdity of how, minutes before, I believed I knew nothing about the experience of joy. But hell, I am the same person who, years ago, was so out of touch that when a roommate left a wadded-up tissue on the floor at the top of our staircase to see what I would do, it sat there for three days. She and I were in disbelief that I walked past and never noticed.

"Joy" might have eluded me the same way I missed that balled-up tissue, but that's not true any longer. My meditation teacher was right. Guidance was right. Joy exists and it has always been available to me.

A short time later, I had an experience that solidified joy's role in my life, helping me to realize joy's unrestrained availability further. During a troubling moment when I worried about paying a bill, a sense of elation rose within me, unexpectedly. I felt an overwhelming sense of relief as if I won the lottery. Yet, in those few seconds, nothing changed concerning my finances. Joy's carefree presence found me because I needed a new perspective. My angst disappeared. I stopped worrying. I felt grateful.

Since then, joy often feels like I'm being washed clean of the gunk that settled in me. No matter how long I feel joy's uplifting presence (sometimes it's only seconds) I feel renewed, lighter, and refreshed. Like Holly Golightly in the movie *Breakfast at Tiffany's,* I too sense, as she did, while peering in the windows at what sparkled, that nothing bad can happen to me when I'm imbued with joy.

Today, there are still times when I fail to understand the punchline of a joke or can't make myself laugh when I'm alone and some mornings the weight of lethargy keeps me in bed. None of those ways I move in the world has changed.

What has changed is my understanding. It's not joy that failed me in those moments, nor have I failed myself. I forgot that joy is available and, therefore, accessible anytime I remember.

Reflections

"Happy" might be an emotion we are more readily able to understand as we attach happiness to an activity, event, or person. But what about joy? Does joy feel a bit elusive, far away, like it did for me? Getting close to joy is simply a matter of understanding your own views about this ever-present gift.

1. How do you relate to joy?
2. Under what circumstances do you experience joy?
3. What might be different about your life if you believed that joy is available right now?

According to Guidance (and the Dalai Lama, by the way), joy is our birthright. Joy is how we are meant to live. Joy means our hearts are open. If this is true, then joy isn't dependent on situations in our life. Joy is an experience we can have by choosing to believe in its existence and its rightful place in our lives.

30. Perfection

The perfection of life is living in the now.

IX

You are perfect, born into perfection because you are you. Your life is perfect just as it is in this moment because you are here in it.

Let go of this idea about perfection, for what it causes can only render you imperfect.

Your trying is enough.

Your willingness is good enough.

Your insistence that you can do better is in your ability, should you decide this.

But that is not perfection; that is choice.

Perfection is only an idea. It is not a requirement.

Trapped at a red light, I fumed at the bozo in front of me because he didn't use his turn signal, and I cursed at the guy in the car ahead of him who drove too slowly. As I waited there, irritated and impatient, my teeth locked in my jaw, my nostrils flared, and my forehead wrinkled like a pug dog.

It took more than a few seconds to admit that I behaved badly. I took a deep breath. I forced a smile. As I let go of my peeved attitude, I softened.

To my horror, I lacked compassion. Maybe the guy who didn't signal had a broken light and couldn't afford to fix it. Maybe the slow guy was a new driver being extra cautious.

Surely, my anger, annoyance, and aggravation harmed others already struggling in a world filled with disharmony. But once again, my surliness blocked the helpful, loving, understanding person I wanted to be.

For many years, I carried a vision of perfection I aspired to become. As a spiritually aware person, I held the idea that, eventually, I would stop getting cross or judgmental or frustrated or aggravated, or . . . the list was long. These days, I am doubtful that I will ever attain this idea of perfection I had for myself.

I'm not perfect now. I expect I never will be in this lifetime. I have emotions that don't always fit with how I would ideally like to act.

When I think about this, I recall a Buddhist nun I met years ago. She confessed that when she crossed over, she would realize how she failed again in her ability to "get it perfect" (she had her own enlightened list) in this incarnation.

I can relate. I imagine my own palm slapping my forehead in disbelief after I'm dead because I didn't perfect this life in the way I imagined for myself.

I'm tied to the mundane emotions that often get the better of me. I tap my foot with impatience as I listen to a girlfriend tell me one more time how she's been hurt by the bastard I told her to leave months ago.

I bark in frustration when I can't open a glass jar. I'm resentful instead of supportive of my husband's decision—a talented musician with a day job—to practice the drums rather than hop off his throne to welcome me home.

I'm not sitting on a mountaintop by myself praying or communing with Guidance every hour of every day. I have to contend with the triggers, challenges, and irritations that arise in my "real" life. Emotions are complicated.

What I can do is increase my awareness. Like that day in my car when my troubling behavior awakened me from a deep sleep.

When I'm disappointed by my actions, I try (sometimes with

and without success) to avoid admonishing myself. Instead, I find grace in my ability to notice how imperfect I am.

On the afternoon I apologized to a store clerk, who I snarled at because of her incompetence, my apology is cause to celebrate. Did I regret flinging her attitude? Sure. I wish I had been perfectly patient in the first place. But what isn't perfect is me and I have to live with that.

Do I promise to act better next time? Yes, but that doesn't mean I follow through on that promise. I am who I am. There is no other me than the one I'm stuck with.

Yet knowing how elusive perfection is helps me to see perfection in everything. This includes the flaws, mistakes, and accidents that exist.

I see this now. I learn from my mistakes as much as from those moments when I've gotten "it" right, so I decided to take Guidance at their word—seeking "change," instead of perfection.

I take comfort knowing that when I fall back into old patterns of anger, disgust, and ridicule—those times when I'm fuming at the nincompoops on the road—staying attentive ensures that I'm one step closer to altering conduct that no longer suits me.

Throughout my life, I have experienced some success with change. Change has enabled me to move past behaviors that cause me great suffering, like my inability to trust people.

I changed my self-diminishing attitude about my imperfect body being a hindrance. While dating, I changed my focus from who I was looking for to who deserved my wonderful qualities. This empowering act brought Johnny, the man I married, who adores and loves me in ways that have far exceeded anything I could have imagined for myself.

I'm still working to change how impatient I am. Real change takes time. This means I often rehash an incident. Being emotionally astute requires investigation. I'm willing to dissect what I feel in order to get to the truth.

Those times, however, when the truth eludes me, it's often an unexpected occurrence that begs me to pay attention. *The Universe's* way of helping because I can't help myself.

When I was diagnosed with Polymyalgia Rheumatica due to the stress of working with people who abused their power, the extreme pain (I couldn't even squeeze a shampoo bottle) forced me to quit my lucrative job.

The suffering proved great. Yet, had it not been for my illness, I never would have discovered how the job was the tipping point to the extreme stress I swallowed from a childhood riddled with abuse. My body absorbed the harmful effects until it finally had had enough. The awareness took me to the depths of the anger and hurt I long denied. I rocked. I wept. I wallowed for days on end. Through my tears, I found my way to healing the long, overdue emotional and physical trauma.

Thanks to Guidance, my experience that change is possible through awareness has been elevated. But Tarot first introduced me to the idea that we can change.

Each of the Major Arcana cards, numbered from zero to twenty-one, highlights what we all have the potential to experience in our lifetime. According to the cards' message, if followed, we will change and grow.

But if you look at the cards in sequence and believe that this growth proceeds in perfect order, then you would be kidding yourself. No matter how neatly each card builds on the other, our lives don't stack up in as orderly a fashion. This means we will probably revisit a card's message more than once. There are layers to our growth.

Like the time I was sure I had changed so much that I could never be in an emotionally abusive relationship again, only to end up living with the next abuser. I revisited that "Devil" card in the Tarot many times before I understood the true cost of being a victim and how that identity impacted many aspects of my life.

Tarot and Guidance only ask that we pay attention to the journey.

Guidance compares the way we change to climbing the Himalayas. Those who take on this massive feat have the tools they need, but that doesn't mean they climb to the summit right away. They remain at various base camp levels, acclimating before their next ascent.

Guidance says we, too, plateau between levels of change until there comes a time when we have assimilated what we learned, ready to move forward and climb again and change even more.

When I look up at the night sky, there is usually one bright star that beckons my attention. I constantly wonder if what I'm seeing is a formed gaseous mass. I've been told it's probably not . . . that what I'm viewing no longer exists. That what I'm staring at is only the light that has remained. That star, with its fleeting impermanence, is my reminder to accept that life is tenuous, rocky, unpredictable, and neither solid nor secure.

I have been taught by Guidance that our flashes of experience represent our true perfection. That, with each breath, we stand in the perfection of our lives, and therefore we exist in perfect accord, at every instant that we walk this earth. In other words, we are the perfection we seek.

I'm emotionally healthier when I accept where I am, not where I think I should be. I can only change what I know, which means I must first be willing to be aware.

I no longer grapple with the notion of perfection. The word and I rarely cross paths. Perfection is as elusive as my understanding of a star that no longer exists as matter. Looking up, however, is what allows me to reflect on that star, and looking inward, is how I change.

242 Guidance from the Universe

Reflections

A gymnast can obtain a "perfect" score; an actor can get every line "perfect;" a ceramicist can throw a "perfect" pot. But these are moments in time that have nothing to do with who these people are. And those who feel they have experienced perfection will probably be unable to reach that perfect moment again. Or perhaps they'll drive themselves ragged trying to replicate what once was. But they, too, can try. Either way, I'm not sure it's humanly possible to be perfect. What do you think?

1. How does the idea of perfection influence you?
2. How would your life be different if you didn't seek perfection?
3. In this moment, if you wholeheartedly accepted your-self, would you then not experience all the joy you are? All the love you hold? All the peace you seek? All the perfection you already are?

I have used the word "perfect" to describe a pizza so delicious that I eat enough slices for three people. I have also uttered the word "perfection" to describe the beauty of sage-colored moss dangling like fine lace from the limbs of an oak tree. In both instances, I defined what "perfect" means to me.

When I look at a map of the world, the obvious conclusion is that those who live where my finger lands on the globe will also decide what perfection means to them. Therefore, is it possible to collectively agree on what "perfection" is?

The question might be a good one to awaken our curiosity. Not only to understand how each of us identifies with perfection but to discover the merits of a word, which, according to the dictionary, defines perfection "as being as free as possible from flaws or defects."

Epilogue

The Path Is Love

When we partner with spirit, many of us think that our lives will smell like roses and that we'll be gifted with unicorns, only to discover those times when our journey feels more like being trapped in a dark, cold cellar without a flashlight. We spiral downward, crushed by our circumstances, instead of feeling uplifted by the tremendous amount of universal love we believe is available to us. Nobody wants more pain in their life.

But that's the thing about the seeker's path. When we begin, despite our good intentions, we can't possibly know what jumping onto a spiritual path might offer.

Years ago, I had a client who came to me on several occasions for a Tarot Guidance reading. She worked with her own wonderful guides, but during a traumatic time, her steadfast belief in the Universe's hand of love unraveled.

In the face of her sudden tragedy, she questioned (as many do when hardship finds us) her steadfast belief in the Universe's benevolent goodness. She felt lost.

When Guidance advised her to stay on the path of pain—to follow wherever that pain led and to walk with her fears instead of running away—she protested. She ditched the path she had been following, even though the road of struggle was right in front of her.

If the Universe was all-caring, she questioned, why would she be in the midst of such an unbearable, intolerable time?

Guidance tried to explain how divine love remains, even when we are faced with challenges and even when those challenges feel insurmountable. What's missing during these horrific periods in our lives isn't love but trust and our faith in whatever the path brings, along with the understanding that we have a choice about how we face those challenges.

Guidance reminds us that tumultuous times are as much a part of our lives as the ease we feel during others. It's not that those difficult challenges are necessary to see the light; it's that the yuk gets our attention. Unfortunately, for most of us, it is the messy stuff that motivates our growth.

Yet many seekers, including me, forget that the journey is simply what shows up, what presents itself, and what life experience comes our way.

Remaining optimistic—seeing ourselves through a lens of love—isn't easy while we sit in the muck of our lives. In my day-to-day life, living in a state of unconditional love is a challenge. I'm not someone who connects to that feeling effortlessly. Love's lightness of being gets clouded by the mistrust, judgments, and fear I carry.

When I'm with Guidance, however, whether it be for myself or a client, it is unconditional love that pulses through me. This unexpected gift erases my limitations. It feels as if I'm intertwined with the greater cosmos where unity is infinite and acceptance is all. I'm free of preconceptions and personal baggage.

Due to my experiences, I have no doubt that love, as Guidance points out, is the truth of our lives. Therefore, my misery can't deny love, and I can't count on happiness to initiate love. Love exists, and tapping into its vastness is my choice.

When I'm unable to make that choice, for whatever reason, I'm the one holding myself back. And I hold myself back more often than I would like.

But to reread Guidance's words is to regain the hope in love and what it offers. Guidance shows us how to direct our path inward. If we want love to grow in our world, it must start with the love we feel for ourselves.

Guidance asked me to make their wisdom public so you could gain insights to sweep away the cobwebs that make it impossible to see your true beauty.

Therefore, the messages in this book are ones you can reread whenever you face any of the topics listed in the Table of Contents that cause you to suffer, feel stuck, or turn you away from loving yourself.

Over the many years I've been offering readings, I've had the good fortune to meet people around the world through social media and my website. And what all seekers have in common is our desire to grow. We are not a complacent bunch.

We are profoundly aware of those times when we are at our wit's end, struggling, trapped by misery we can't shake. Our grace is that we want to rise above our dissatisfaction, so we look for answers.

Guidance offers answers, but it is up to each of us to decide whether what they say resonates because being true to ourselves is the way forward.

Use this book to discover your truth. Always remember that you are at the center of the circle. Your life is the one that's most precious, and your life is the one that matters. Self-love is not a selfish act. Do not worry that prioritizing self-care will diminish your care for others. That can't happen.

What can happen and will happen by reading Guidance's words is that you will improve the loving relationship with yourself. As we all know, healing starts with the kindness we show ourselves. This is a personal benefit that enhances everyone because when we feel good, we do better for others. And if we all feel better, perhaps there's a chance the world can also heal.

The potent messages from Guidance in this book make that possibility more attainable.

For now, however, being self-aware and mindful is what we individually must do to continue walking love's path. The hope—for me, you, and anyone else who cares to listen—is that each time we tap into the love that naturally exists, the greater our chances of being the love that Guidance insists we already are.

There is no greater gift than the life you've been given.
We see you in all the ways you are, and we love you.
All we ask is that you love you too.

The Tarot Cards Chosen
for Each Chapter

I decided to use Tarot cards to reflect each topic. I did this because, whether you are familiar with Tarot or not, visuals are powerful. Pictures can illicit messages that words cannot.

Tarot is not an exact science. There is no definitive explanation for how Tarot works or why it is so accurate. Yet we do know that reading the Tarot offers us the opportunity to broaden our intuitive skills, to trust what we see in the cards, and to allow the images themselves to tell us their story.

Our ability to free-associate and use our "hits" to guide us struck me when I taught Tarot. As the class gathered in my living room for the evening's curriculum on spreads, we shuffled the cards and then arranged them on my coffee table.

Each participant took turns analyzing the ten cards that lay before us. Nobody had the same interpretation. Yet, each person came up with worthy messages that made sense and taught us a great deal about the situation at hand. This intuitive way of reading the cards came after these students had all learned the same definitions.

There is no doubt that a formal study of the Tarot is important. But for the most part, I think of the Tarot the same way saxophonist Charlie Parker thought about jazz when he said, "First you learn the instrument, then you learn the music, then you forget all that shit and just play."

For this book, I used the Rider-Waite-Smith deck. Although I know each card's recommended definitions intimately, here, I relied on my intuition to guide my pick for every chapter. What I chose is an abstraction.

Perhaps when you read what I wrote, you will recognize what I saw and understand my decision. Or maybe you won't agree. If the latter is true for you, it gives me great pleasure to think you might have chosen different cards. If you have a deck, I encourage you to pick the cards you prefer. Should you try this, I would be delighted for you to share your results with me.

Chapter 1: Awareness—IX The Hermit. We are called to wake up and look inward. This awareness enables us to see ourselves and others more clearly.

Chapter 2: Emotions—XVIII The Moon. The female attribute of the moon uncovers emotions that lay deep within us. When we bring our feelings forward, we can learn to embrace them.

Chapter 3: Anger—Five of Wands. When we attach our anger to another person, we often leave conflict in its wake. But anger's truth isn't about the impact it leaves on others as much as the impact it leaves on us.

Chapter 4: Surrender—Four of Swords. By surrendering to what is, we have given ourselves permission to relax. In repose, our struggles subside. We are in the flow of our lives, unencumbered, able to hear what we could not hear before.

Chapter 5: Hope—Six of Cups. As children, we are initially naïve, full of hope and possibility.

Chapter 6: Letting Go—Four of Wands. Letting go takes courage and enables us to experience the peace we are seeking.

Chapter 7: Jealousy—Five of Swords. When we feel jealous, we often obsess about wanting to be like someone else or wanting what someone else has. But we do this at a cost to ourselves.

Chapter 8: Gratitude—XXI The World. The grace of gratitude can move every mountain we encounter.

Chapter 9: Money—Six of Pentacles. Money flows in and out of our lives. We are both the receiver and the giver of money. It is good to remember this.

Chapter 10: Intuition—II The High Priestess. Our internal voice speaks through us. Recognizing this unshakable knowing prompts us to pay attention.

Chapter 11: Acceptance—Two of Cups. The wise person chooses acceptance instead of being pushed and pulled by the discord of opposites.

Chapter 12: Failure and Success—Eight of Wands. We can allow failure and success to define the ups and downs of our journey, or we can define for ourselves how these two events affect us.

Chapter 13: Religion and God—XII The Hanged Man. As seekers, clarifying our understanding of spirituality and its meaning is a noble cause worth contemplating.

Chapter 14: Judgment—XI Justice. Ponder what purpose and under what conditions justice is served when judgments are present.

Chapter 15: Worry—Seven of Cups. Worry can become an overwhelming fixation that focuses our attention on the past or the future while affecting our present.

Chapter 16: Comparison—Three of Cups. When we stop comparing, we stand in our own power, imbue self-trust and self-reliance, and can celebrate ourselves and others.

Chapter 17: Death—XIII Death. Death is part of the life cycle. Therefore, gleaning death's lessons while we're alive may prove valuable.

Chapter 18: Grief—Three of Swords. The pain of grief follows us. Allowing for all expressions of grief proves to be a healthy release.

Chapter 19: Abundance—XVII The Star. Acknowledging abundance is a nourishing act that affects the entirety of our lives.

Chapter 20: Choice—Two of Wands. Choice equals freedom. To recognize this means we can embrace what comes our way without stress.

Chapter 21: Fear—Nine of Swords. When fear takes hold, look at it and name it so the fear will lessen.

Chapter 22: Forgiveness—Ten of Cups. The act of forgiveness lifts burdens, lightening our hearts and everyone else's.

Chapter 23: Loss—Five of Cups. Loss has the potential to turn our attention toward possibility.

Chapter 24: Sadness and Sorrow—Eight of Cups. Acknowledging sadness and sorrow can point our direction toward better days.

Chapter 25: Shame—Four of Cups. When we sit with shame, it is nearly impossible to recognize any gifts being offered to us.

Chapter 26: Time—X Wheel of Fortune. Time marks the ups and downs, the backward look, and the forward motion of our lives. But the truth of time is to notice how, in each moment, we are where we are.

Chapter 27: Faith—0 The Fool. Every step we take with faith might feel risky but has the potential to lead us to safety regardless of where we end up.

Chapter 28: Suffering—Ten of Wands. We often carry the heavy burden of suffering far longer than we need to.

Chapter 29: Joy—XIX The Sun. By standing in our light and the light of the Universe, we feel joy wash over us.

Chapter 30: Perfection—Nine of Pentacles. We are already the perfection we seek. We ought to be enthralled and enchanted with who we are.

Feel free to reach out to me through my website—I'd love to hear from you! Visit www.jillamysager.com or scan the QR Code.

Acknowledgments

The act of writing is solitary, but editing begs for many eyes. I want to thank my readers who, over the years, gave their time and honest feedback as I authored my stories. All of you are gifted, talented women who made me a better writer. Alice Tallmadge, Cathleen Wilder, Sarah Wayland, and JoJo Jensen—you are all great friends, and I love you.

To Anne Kerman for picking up the phone every time I needed her and whose gentle encouragement helped me beyond what her humble soul will ever be able to acknowledge, as I can hear her saying, "I didn't do a thing." But she's wrong about that.

To Catherine J. Rourke, my editor and fellow "Bronxite," who offered her skills, support, and soulful, loving nature to make this book even better. Meeting you was meant to be, but becoming friends was the greater gift.

Big thanks to Tabitha Lahr whose artful vision for this book far exceeded my expectations.

To all the women at She Writes Press I offer my grateful heart, with a special shout out to Shannon Green for her patience and attention during all the tasks leading up to this book's publication. With all she had to do, she made what I had to do much easier. Thank you.

Receiving messages from the Universe took me by surprise, but I wouldn't have been as ready if not for three trailblazing women who showed me it was possible.

To Claudia Leone for her loving, nonjudgmental presence in the world and for hosting weekly sessions where the information she channeled was a revelation to this skeptic, yet the support from her guides made me a believer.

To Ann White, who took me under her wing, insisting I, too, had her channeling abilities. At that time, I didn't believe her pronouncement because I didn't believe in myself. But what Ann predicted those many years ago came true.

To Belleruth Naparstek for her important book, *Your Sixth Sense: Unlocking the Power of Your Intuition* (HarperOne/Harper-Collins, 1997). I had been receiving Guidance's information for a few years when a friend bought me the book. Chapter after chapter highlighted how people become highly intuitive, and unbeknownst to me, much of what Ms. Naparstek wrote did, in fact, describe my journey, giving me permission to accept what I had been experiencing.

My thanks to all these amazing women will never be enough, but by honoring them here, I hope I have captured their profound impact on my life.

And finally, to Johnny. Your faith in my ability kept me writing, and so did those weekend eggs over easy. I love you more.

About the Author

J ill Amy Sager is a highly sought-after Tarot reader, channeler, and public speaker with an international following. Physically disabled since birth, she spent many years with low self-esteem. Her life was transformed thanks to Tarot and wisdom from the Universe—an experience that has inspired her to dedicate her practice to helping others. This honest approach has brought her popular acclaim. Once a professional hand drum teacher and drum circle facilitator, Jill is also the author of *Beginning Hand Drumming: A Guide to Recreation and Wellness*, touted as the go-to instructional by former Janis Joplin drummer Dave Getz. When she isn't with a client or writing, you'll find her hanging out with friends and family. She lives in Western Oregon.

Author photo © Leah Nansel, Flint and Flame Photography

Looking for your next great read?

We can help!

Visit www.shewritespress.com/next-read
or scan the QR code below for a list
of our recommended titles.

She Writes Press is an award-winning
independent publishing company founded to
serve women writers everywhere.